EVOLUTION _to_ PURPOSE

CHOOSING
A LIFE OF
AUTHENTICITY
WITH WORK

BRYAN HONG, PhD

NEW GROUNDING PRESS

Lenexa

New Grounding Press

ISBN 979-8-9872610-0-2 (paperback edition)
ISBN 979-8-9872610-1-9 (ebook edition)
ISBN 979-8-9872610-2-6 (audiobook edition)

Library of Congress Control Number: 2023905313

Publisher's Cataloging-in-Publication data

Names: Hong, Bryan, author.
Title: Evolution to purpose : choosing a life of authenticity with work / Bryan Hong, PhD.
Description: Includes bibliographical references. | Lenexa, KS: New Grounding Press, 2023.
Identifiers: LCCN: 2023905313 | ISBN: 979-8-9872610-0-2 (paperback) | 979-8-9872610-1-9 (ebook) | 979-8-9872610-2-6 (audio)
Subjects: LCSH Job satisfaction. | Occupations--Psychological aspects. | Job stress. | Stress (Psychology) | Psychology, Industrial. | Work--Psychological aspects. | Employees--Attitudes. | Employee motivation. | Work-life balance. | BISAC BUSINESS & ECONOMICS / Careers / Job Hunting | PSYCHOLOGY / Movements / Transpersonal | PSYCHOLOGY / Movements / Existential | EDUCATION / Counseling / Career Development | SELF-HELP / Personal Growth / Happiness
Classification: LCC HF5549.5.J63 .H66 2023 | DDC 158.7--dc23

All names and identifying characteristics of former students have been changed to protect the privacy of the individuals involved. The content in this book is for informational purposes, and is not meant to substitute professional advice.

Book cover design by Fiaz Ahmed
Editing by Lisa Kramer
Book interior design by Ashley Halsey (paperback)
Printed in the United States of America

First printing May 2023

To my wife, and to my students who opened my eyes.

AUTHOR'S NOTE

If you work in education, you can see something in your students that most others in society don't notice. When you get to know them well enough, you can catch a glimpse of their potential, what they are perhaps meant to become. Our only real job as teachers is to see them get closer to realizing this potential, and to have only their interests at heart. This is almost completely at odds with what the rest of the world does.

After graduation, my students were surrounded by people who constantly judged their value based on how useful they were for their personal needs or to their organizations, which are very narrow definitions of value. This wasn't to say their workplaces were all unpleasant—many liked the people they worked with. But it's also true they usually paid little attention to what my students were meant to become as individuals. And, they didn't make much effort to support their true growth and potential, unless by coincidence it was in their interest to do so. This is an understandable part of life at work. But if your job is to help people realize their unique potential, it's difficult to conclude that all is well with the way our education system works, especially after years of seeing firsthand what happens to your former students. And my students are not alone. Clear signs indicate we have a problem.

At the time of this writing, our world is experiencing a period of dramatic social change, which is transforming our understanding of work. Many are choosing to quit or disengage from their jobs, the sum of which reflects a form of rebellion against our current social structure. Like similar periods throughout human history, very different interpretations are being told of what is happening, which to some extent reflects differences between the perspectives of the older and younger generations. A common narrative from those who are older is this: The younger generation's unhealthy degree of entitlement and distaste for the status quo demonstrates a lack of wisdom and maturity. Those who are younger ask: Why have we accepted our society the way it is, with all its problems and unsatisfying answers to how we are supposed to live? These different perspectives will eventually reach a resolution. When that happens, if the conclusion is that the old answers are no longer acceptable, they can no longer be the answers. But rebellions fail to create meaningful change for the better if those rebelling don't understand the true nature of the problem they want to solve. We must know why the problem exists to begin with, which requires understanding how the machinery of our imperfect world works. Until we know this, the victory of our current rebellion—or any future rebellion—remains uncertain.

I've taught in business schools throughout my academic career, and my courses are usually about competitive strategy, which explains why some companies succeed while others don't. Early on in my career as a professor, I discovered most of my students who wanted to meet privately with me in my office were much more interested in discussing their career paths than the content I was teaching them in class. For reasons I only partially understand, I became a popular person to reach out to for advice. My students eventually encompassed those younger and older, including undergraduates, full-time MBAs who returned to school to earn a graduate degree, and part-time MBAs who were older professionals attending night and weekend classes. Conversations about career concerns inevitably became bigger conversations about life concerns, and I began to notice patterns with the challenges my students faced. These patterns were the first pieces I could clearly see inside a much larger machine at work: the mechanics of how our world shapes us.

The goal of this book is not to motivate you, although once you've reached the end of it you may feel the need to change something about what you're doing. Even if you're feeling discouraged and lost, which is understandable if you've picked up a book about purpose, the real problem is not actually a lack of motivation. Rather, the problem is a lack of awareness—not seeing fully the way things work in the external world and inside ourselves. This book is meant to try and help you navigate through life a bit more like someone who has learned how to be a better driver who can skillfully handle the road ahead of them, instead of only being able to drive well enough to not destroy their vehicle. I've worked in education long enough to know our system doesn't really teach people how to drive well in life, even though it would greatly improve so many things in our world if only we did. Both literally and figuratively, we all come to forks in the road where we must make choices that will ultimately define who we will become. We must make these choices regardless of whether or not we know what we're doing. While seeing more clearly usually isn't the difference between life and death during these moments, it is often the difference between never knowing how much more we could have been and becoming the best version of ourselves.

A friend who read an early draft of this book argued that

purpose can't make one happier for very long because happiness is fleeting. Indeed, a quick search online of the expression had no shortage of articles attesting to just how fleeting happiness is. A little more searching (and academic literature reading) revealed that many people, psychologists and philosophers included, use the term happiness to mean different things. In this book, the term "happiness" doesn't refer to something fleeting, but to a more stable and longer-lasting feeling. Fulfillment would be a close synonym. Purpose is an important component of this happiness in life.[1] I would guess everyone I know who isn't a psychologist or philosopher would also call this feeling happiness. You can call it whatever you like. I am much more concerned you feel it in the first place.

A standard approach many of my academic colleagues take to writing books is to dig deep into all the scientific studies on a topic, then summarize their findings in the most exciting way they can think of. That is not the approach taken here, nor is this meant to be that kind of book. This book reflects my own personal observations, thoughts, and insights, many of which are based on conversations I've had with my students over the years. The ideas in this book began to form during my first academic job at Ivey Business School in Canada, and crystallized while I was at The Wharton School of the University of Pennsylvania (Wharton) and New York University (NYU). I wrote this book more as an educator than anything else, as someone who works in the system and wishes to share what they see.

At different points throughout the book, I highlight the importance of self-reflection, but don't discuss in detail what self-reflection actually looks like. Discussing this topic at the level of depth it deserves is a book on its own, but the reality is, there is no one best way to do it, and what works for each of us is highly personal. My approach is to meditate sitting with my eyes closed in silence, observing my breath. I aim for an hour each day, but there are many days where I feel lucky to squeeze in twenty minutes, which is the minimum I'd recommend if you've never tried it before. I know others who go running, do yoga, write in a journal, walk in nature, or engage in other types of physical exercise, but this list is hardly exhaustive. What all of these activities have in common is an increased focus on the self and the removal of outside distractions—the opinions of people around us, gossip, work meetings, background noise, e-mails, social media, smartphones, television, traffic, to-do lists... Find what works for you, and know that what you begin to see, including the things you wish you didn't see, is the person we all want to know. I mean it. You just don't realize it yet.

Bryan Hong
January 21, 2023

CONTENTS

PART II
Evolution

INTRODUCTION

Why are so many people unhappy at work, if they choose the work they do? In my corporate working life before entering academia, I never found anyone who truly understood the answer. Many around me believed that unhappiness at work was a natural part of life, especially if one wanted to make a decent living. It was the best one could do because it was the most life was willing to offer. But I knew this answer was false—I saw people who genuinely enjoyed the work they did, even if they were few and far between. What I couldn't understand was what separated them from the unhappy majority. The difference wasn't the jobs they did or their abilities, or even the amount of money they made. From what I could see at the time, being happy at work seemed to be a phenomenon that randomly blessed a lucky few, much like winning the lottery. It was only later, when I left the corporate world to become a professor, that I began to see there was nothing natural or random about why the world looked this way.

As a professor, I regularly met many new people each semester in my classroom, most of whom were thinking about what they wanted to do with their lives. My students came from diverse backgrounds, and because I taught both undergraduates and graduate students, they ranged from young adults in their twenties to those fast approaching the middle of their lives. I had young idealists, older jaded cynics, and everyone in between. Some were philosophers who asked "Why?" all the time, while others were soldiers who never asked why but dutifully marched down the road in front of them. The many office visits and phone calls from my students seeking advice over the years, both before and after graduation, allowed me to see their progression, including both challenges and triumphs. A nagging feeling grew inside me as time went by, which refused to go away. Something wasn't right.

Adrian the Overachiever

Adrian was an undergraduate student of mine who was the kind of student schools love to celebrate: she earned consistently outstanding grades, was well-liked and respected by her classmates, and did it all without a sense of entitlement or arrogance. During her first visit to my office, her youthful optimism radiated throughout the room. Wearing one of her many bright-colored t-shirts and skinny designer jeans, her eyes quickly scanned my office and noted my choice of décor, which included a set of fake plants to provide a calming energy for students who came to argue about their grades.

After asking a few basic questions about my life before academia, she paused for a brief moment, and her normally confident demeanor faded slightly. I could tell she was unsure about whether to say her next words. Maybe she wasn't sure I was the right person to talk to. Or maybe she had to find the courage to say what was on her mind. Or maybe both.

"How are we supposed to know what to do with our lives?" she asked.

My brow furrowed for a split second. She clearly hadn't come to ask about my course. I was in the early years of my job as a professor, and still had the unrealistic expectation that my students would only ask me questions about what I taught them in class. "You don't feel like you know?"

"No, not really. I keep going to these recruiting events held by different companies and everyone seems nice, but I don't feel like I'm getting closer to knowing what I should do."

She had a point. I had been an undergraduate student too, long ago, and also went to business school. But for some reason I never noticed what Adrian saw. She couldn't have realized then the true nature of the problem she faced, but at least she could sense there was one.

"Don't worry too much about it," I said. "You're not supposed to have all the answers right now." I knew this was unhelpful advice, but at the time didn't know what else to say. The truth was, I was told the same thing at various points throughout my own life, by my professors, successful businesspeople I admired, and even a career counselor, and I thought at the time this constituted the best wisdom anybody had. The next-best career advice I ever received was from one of my favorite professors as an undergraduate who told me to "just be happy," but gave no guidance on how exactly to do it. If I repeated the same words to Adrian, I knew it would only prove to her she had come to the wrong person. And maybe she had. Nothing I learned earning my PhD degree at Berkeley, or during the rest of my years of education, had trained me to help my students with this.

After our meeting, Adrian would be given every opportunity, every signal of being wanted and highly valued that her world could offer. Everything seemed to go her way. She received a job offer from virtually every employer she interviewed with, and made it look easy. She accepted an offer from a prestigious global investment bank, which had worked particularly hard to court her once she received the job offer. By all accounts, she had a promising career ahead of her, and arguably represented the best of what was possible for those who attended our school. As the years passed after her graduation, evidence of her achievements only grew as she took on more senior roles, moving from one prestigious firm to another and earning significantly more money each year. From the outside, Adrian had an amazing life, perhaps the best life anyone could hope to achieve in her world. She had also become an inspiring role model for others.

There's just one problem with Adrian's story: her life during those years didn't feel nearly as great to her as what you might be imagining. While her intellect and work ethic made her more than capable of doing the jobs she did, they didn't make her experiences more meaningful or enjoyable. The reality was that most of her days during those years were miserable. She had initially hoped the periods of misery would only be temporary, but bad days often became bad weeks, or even bad months. When her hope permanently dissolved she would leave for another job elsewhere, only to find misery waiting for her again. A few months after starting at one of these new jobs, I spoke to her on the phone.

"Well, at least I don't have to work as many hours," she said. The optimism and energy she once had in my office years ago had largely faded by now, replaced by a hint of cold resignation in her voice.

"That's the best thing you have to say about your new job?" I asked, astonished.

"The money's good, too," she said. "I have a nice view from my office. Really nice, actually. And I like my assistant. She's nice." She was trying to sound positive, but knew I wasn't convinced. She wasn't either, which led her to a different line of argument to make sense of her predicament. "I don't think you can get everything you want in life. I'm just making the best of it," she said.

"Sure, but this is not about trying to get everything you want. It's about the fact you've been miserable for years now. The situation you're in, it isn't happening because you didn't work hard enough or aren't smart enough. You've figured out by now this isn't about that."

But what had Adrian done wrong? It seemed she had done everything right, given the values and lessons we had taught her. In her world she was someone whose status was highly valued, an example of success for others to follow. But despite her impressive accomplishments and the money she earned, she was undeniably miserable. Why was she miserable? The fact that our phone conversation was at 9:00 p.m.—the only time she knew she would be free, at the end of her workday—probably didn't help. She had little time or energy left in her life for herself, let alone family or friends. Our previous conversation had been in person at a trendy cafe, where her appearance was a contradiction of fresh, designer-label clothes and the weary look of someone who hadn't slept well in days, with her eyes anxiously glancing at her phone for messages throughout our meeting. She had remarked then how quickly the years seemed to pass by since graduation, and yet she had very few memories of life outside of work that she could recall. But as miserable as she was, I knew the cause of her misery wasn't as simple as the job itself—I knew others who were much happier doing the same type of work. She had also been proactive in switching jobs to be happier, and yet happiness seemed to constantly elude her. Over time, I would discover Adrian's story would be far more common than I could possibly have imagined, and it had nothing to do with one's capabilities, effort, or achievements. Adrian ultimately felt no different at work than many of her former classmates; the only difference was many of her classmates believed she must surely be happier than they were.

What We Didn't Teach You

The nagging feeling I had after seeing Adrian and my other students was, in retrospect, the result of a shift in my own awareness. What my students all had in common was a desire to feel good about the work they did, and to find fulfillment in doing it. Their efforts to answer the different questions and challenges they faced all reflected their intention to get there, the best way they knew how. But rather than being well-prepared by us—the education system—to make their decisions, they were struggling. I could see where their struggles reflected lessons we failed to teach, and where their employers would be of little help to guide them. Being in a business school probably did not help; I couldn't think of which course, which department in the school, would have told them what they needed to know in order to find what they wanted. They weren't bad students who had failed to heed the wisdom given to them; the problem was we hadn't given it to them in the first place. This would have been easier to brush aside if the challenges my students faced were minor topics our education system had overlooked, the result of the need to prioritize much more relevant subjects. But these were some of the most crucial decisions my students would make in their lives, which would define much of their future. What was more important than that?

The topics discussed in this book would have been part of a class you had in school, if our education system worked the way it should. The pursuit of happiness is not easy even if one truly understands the challenge, but the starting point most of us are given is the equivalent of being forced to march forward in darkness, with no light to illuminate the way. With so many blindly moving forward, finding happiness at work really can seem like being the lucky winner of a lottery. My students understandably struggled the same way so many others do, stumbling forward in the dark. But we don't have to pray for luck to be happier; we just need more light to see.

PART I

Living with the Machine

1

A LIFE OF HAPPINESS
AND PURPOSE

Happiness requires action. Action requires direction.
If only we knew the way...
~ Anonymous

If you've chosen what you want to do for work, why do you think you'll be happy doing it? And, what if you realize later you aren't happy? The second question arises when the answer to the first question is proven incorrect, and if it seems obvious that the answer to being unhappy is to quit and do something you'd enjoy more, then you are either a true maverick or lucky enough to have not yet encountered this dilemma in your own life. When many of us eventually face this situation—some of us multiple times throughout our lives—dealing with it is rarely so straightforward. The truth is, many of us make changes that aren't effective, or don't make any changes at all. This happens so frequently in our society it's often thought of as normal, although it reflects a widespread problem. What's the problem? Not understanding how happiness at work is a combined result of what we believe we are able to do with our lives, and how well we know ourselves. And the implications of this go far beyond how we feel at work, because the root of this problem also shapes what the other branches of our life look like—our family life, who we choose as friends, and how we understand our role in the universe. It defines how we experience every part of our life.

Our Choices Reflect Our Beliefs About What We Think Is Possible, But Not Necessarily What We Actually Want

When we choose the work we do, our decision always reflects a mixture of what we want to do with our life and what we believe is possible for us, but our choices are often guided more by what we believe is possible. Our understanding of what we can do is often what really shapes our path. I've had many students tell me what they wanted to do with their lives, only to find out later what they really shared was only what they believed they were capable of doing. This might seem like a sensible approach, except no one—including us—actually knows where the boundary is of what's possible in our life. We really don't know what we're capable of, and neither does anybody else. This is how life itself is designed. The limit of our potential—what we would look like if we were the best version of ourselves—is a mystery each of us must solve on our own.

Because the boundary of what's possible for us is unknown, our beliefs about what we can do usually come from the many messages we receive from the external world that judges us, and from observing what others around us achieve. These beliefs begin to form long before we reach adulthood, and are heavily influenced by who we have as role models—often members of our family—and their own beliefs. All of this is reasonable to a degree, but it's also very limiting. Depending on our beliefs, we may conclude that what we really want to do in life isn't possible for us, which greatly diminishes our chances of experiencing happiness with work. We may change employers or jobs, but ultimately be no better off because the possibilities our beliefs lead us to are too narrow to expect anything better. This is how many of my students lived—bright and talented, but with a set of beliefs that made their world too small to be happy.

Living a life of limited beliefs doesn't mean our beliefs are true, however; it only proves that beliefs shape our lives. If we see someone do what we originally thought was impossible or unrealistic, our beliefs change and our sense of possibility expands. This happens all the time, but can be difficult to accept if our daily environment is dominated by those who embrace and enforce limited beliefs. Ironically, this is why pursuing what we want to do can be a much better way to learn what we're capable of doing in life instead of limiting ourselves to what we believe is possible in any given moment. The trials of experience are a much better teacher than following limited beliefs, and our chances of experiencing happiness at work are much greater. But reaching the limit of our potential isn't just about discovering what's possible to achieve in the world we live in; it's also about the discovery that takes place inside us.

Our True Self and What Purpose Really Means

Somewhere inside us is a version of ourselves that is our authentic, true self. This is not an imaginary philosophical idea. Your true self is real. It may seem obvious we should know who this person is, but the reality is many of us don't. We may not bother to take a long enough look in the mirror to get to know this self. Or, maybe we don't want to. Maybe nobody told us why it would matter if we did. But this person is the essence of the best version of ourselves. Not knowing this true self well enough is one reason why we may struggle to see what we could, or should, become. Our true self has its own values, its own opinion about what it wants, and insists on having its own particular needs met. Doing what we want with our lives in the true sense and experiencing happiness with work requires getting to know and supporting our true self.

This book is about finding and having purpose in your working life. Purpose serves as the bridge between the external world, with all of its possibilities and challenges, and the world inside us, where our true self resides. Without it, we are unable to connect the two worlds, and must carry the burden of constantly negotiating the demands of both sides to manage the gap between them, while never being able to fully satisfy either. This state of disconnection is why we can easily work hard to accomplish difficult, impressive-sounding goals in the external world and yet feel no joy or real satisfaction once they've been achieved. We can achieve victory, receive extravagant rewards, and have a magnificent parade where we are celebrated by many others. We then lead the parade toward the world inside us, where our true self lives, to deliver the joy and satisfaction of victory. But along the way, the parade is stopped at the edge of the external world because it cannot cross to where our true self is. This matters because the triumphs of the external world mean nothing to the inner world if there is no bridge to connect them. This disconnection is also why we may feel exhausted emotionally if we constantly have to dismiss or restrict what our true self wants to say or do. Our true self seeks to act freely in the external world, but needs a bridge to get there. Even if we don't know what the best version of ourselves looks like, we do know that person has somehow figured out how to successfully connect their life in the external world with their true self, to exist with purpose. This is what a life of authenticity with work looks like.

What exactly do I mean by **purpose**, though? In our working life, a sense of purpose is a feeling of *profound knowing why you are doing what you are doing at work, coupled with the belief that the work you do is an important expression of your true self.* Purpose touches a much deeper part of the human psyche—the part of us that isn't easy to see when others look at us. It is also highly personal. It doesn't matter at all whether someone else sees what you do and judges you to have purpose. *It matters tremendously whether you look at yourself in the mirror and judge yourself to have purpose.*

The reason why having a strong sense of purpose at work matters is because of how much it contributes to our quality of life. Virtually all of us spend an extraordinary amount of our lives working, often much more of our lifetime than with our loved ones and friends. This puts a heavy weight on how work makes us feel as human beings. If we have a strong sense of purpose in our work, we feel empowered and happier. But purpose doesn't just help us feel better; it also opens a path to a different way of understanding and living life, a different kind of existence—a means to becoming the best version of ourselves.

The Challenge of Finding Purpose

It would be nice to think everyone eventually finds their purpose, and that simply letting life take its course will lead us there. But you already know that's not true. Many people never find it, but this is not because it doesn't exist. For almost everyone, finding purpose is the consequence of an intentional, conscious process. If you're not looking for it or don't know how to find it, it's not likely to appear. If finding your purpose was as easy as figuring out your favorite flavor of ice cream, an entire book on the subject wouldn't be necessary because little self-reflection or knowledge would be needed to figure out the answer. Finding your purpose is a little more complicated than that. And it turns out our society isn't really designed to help you find it, either. It's designed for something else, a different goal in mind. Working in higher education, I came to see this clearly after years of being at the end of the production line, just before my students transitioned into the next stage of their lives.

Seeing Clearly to Build the Bridge

If there's an overarching intention I have for this book, it's to help you see more clearly as you move forward in your life. Finding purpose is about navigating the external world and the world inside you to build the bridge between them. You need to see well enough in order to navigate, and to know where and how to build the bridge. Leading a great victory parade without clarity will surely take you somewhere, but probably not where your true self is valued. But with greater clarity, you might see whether you are going in the right or wrong direction, or maybe you'll see parts of yourself you've never noticed before. You might realize the job you've been aiming for doesn't fit well with your true self. Or, you may become aware that your true self is far more interesting and complicated than what you've been told your whole life, with its own unique needs and interests no one else has noticed. Whatever you see, seeing it clearly will be essential.

A core premise of this book is that knowing how the machinery of the external world works to shape us will already take you much of the way to finding your own purpose. The machinery includes systemic and deeply rooted forces embedded in the structure of our society that will try to nudge you in certain directions. This is because the external world already has an opinion about what you should be doing with your life, based on what it thinks it knows about you. The problem is, of course, it doesn't really know you. This is further complicated by the fact that we often don't really know ourselves, either. If we don't see this situation clearly, the judgment of the external world can easily become our reality, simply because we don't realize we are following a road someone else has chosen for us. It is an existence without being fully conscious, with enough unfulfilling distractions to keep us from our true path to last a lifetime. Many of my students believed these distractions would be enough to satisfy them, only to discover the truth later. But another way forward, another road, is open: we can choose the path of purpose, and evolve beyond the machinery that shapes us.

2

HOW PURPOSE LEADS TO SUCCESS IN LIFE

The secret of success is constancy to purpose.
~ Benjamin Disraeli

How does one succeed in life? I often ask my undergraduate students this question on our first day of class, and deliberately keep the question vague because I want to understand what they believe about success. One can learn a lot about someone's values and view of the world by letting them fill in the blanks. Our discussion is usually the first time anyone has ever asked them this question, even though they are close to graduation by the time they arrive in my classroom. My students usually respond by giving predictable answers they believe could never be wrong in a business school class, like knowing the right people and working hard. That's the less interesting part of the exercise. The more interesting part is to see whether anyone asks what the definition of success is *supposed to be*. Only one student in the entire room needs to raise their hand to ask this, so one might think this happens every time. After all, how can we talk about success if we haven't clearly defined it? But I've had many classes where it never occurs to anyone to ask.

The True Definition of Success

My students usually think I'm asking them how people become rich, even though I never use this word in my question. But the truth is that success and failure are concepts created entirely in the mind. Money is simply what most of my students choose as their measure, and the fact that not everyone chooses it illustrates the point. If you don't believe me, every time you experience massive success or catastrophic failure go to a completely different environment where no one would understand or care about what you do, or about the kind of experiences you label as successes or failures. If you visit a remote Buddhist temple for a meditation retreat, try telling the monks how you got promoted at work and received a big pay raise, and see how truly impressed they are. Or begin climbing Mount Everest, and on the way up tell your Sherpa how you received a mediocre bonus because you don't get along with your boss. Of course, it sounds bizarre to even suggest these things, let alone actually do them. Success and failure, and the degree to which you feel them, are purely a product of your mind. It may feel quite real because we are usually surrounded by others who use the same definitions, but even then, it's not an objective truth. There is actually no such thing as success or failure in reality, other than what we believe in our minds.

Given this, we can define what success really means in our world. Success is the achievement of anything that allows us to call ourselves a successful person. Because this differs based on the individual, successful people aren't defined then by any universal standard of achievement, but by whether they feel successful based on their own standard. This might sound strange at first, because we have built so many institutions in our society with the supposed authority to judge our success. Surely, they must be correct in judging us? But one's feeling is the only definition of a successful person that can be true. If the rest of the world thinks of you as an amazing success but you feel like a failure, it's not really true that you're a success. The whole reason for attaining success is to *feel* successful. There is no other worthwhile reason. If humans were supposed to accomplish things only to not feel successful, we'd need to seriously reconsider how we operate as a species, because we're doing something terribly wrong. Genuinely successful people are people who judge themselves to be a success, and feel successful. No other definition makes any sense.

If success is a creation of our minds, then it may seem as if it's completely arbitrary, and that all of us could declare ourselves a success overnight and be better off for it. And that would be a remarkable transformation, if only it worked. Even if it's a product of our minds, the way we determine success cannot be easily changed. It is rooted deep within us, and almost always goes back to conditioning we received in childhood, where we may have learned rewards and good emotions were directly related to achieving certain types of outcomes. Often a quick way to weaken these beliefs at least temporarily is what I mentioned earlier: surround yourself with completely different people who don't share your definition of success and failure, or better yet, don't even bother using these words regularly in their lives. For example, if we grow up measuring our success based on what we achieve according to society's standards, attending gatherings focused on true spiritual growth can often work because they focus on a much deeper understanding of what really matters in life, instead of what those around us might personify. This works because we are taught either through implicit or explicit messaging that success is not something we have the right to define for ourselves. We are told that someone else must define it for us, and being around others who also believe this helps to convince us it must certainly be true. But it isn't true, and it never was.

The Conditions for True Success

If I asked my students to go out into the world and interview every successful person they could find to discover what they all had in common, it's likely they would ask the richest people they knew. They may also look for those who have power and fame. Maybe the answers they gave in my class discussion would be validated—perhaps it really is all about knowing the right people and working long hours that got them to where they are. But the criteria they'd use doesn't exactly select the right people to interview if one wants to understand true success. If it did, it would have to be true that all wealthy, powerful, and famous people in our world go through life feeling remarkably successful, but this isn't true at all. Again, successful people must feel like they are successful for it to be true. So, the right way to find people to interview would be to look for everyone in the world who feels successful. Nothing more is required. And if one did this, they would indeed find things they have in common.

The feeling of success requires that something be accomplished to a certain level of satisfaction. If you watch runners participating in a marathon, you'll notice a wide range of finishing times. But if you look closer, the satisfaction of each participant also varies widely. The second-place runner may be disappointed and consider their performance a failure because they finished after the first-place runner, despite their exceptional achievement.[2] The runner who finished in last place may feel wildly successful and proud of themselves because they proved they are capable of finishing a marathon, which they previously never believed they could do. There may even be runners who didn't finish the race but are satisfied because they had the courage to try. Again, the definition of success here is entirely a product of the mind. But for all of those who walk away feeling successful, success is directly related to having done something well enough.

But simply accomplishing something isn't enough to feel successful. It must also be true that there is a sense of importance about what's being done. If you leave your home and check your mailbox, you may not feel very successful no matter how well you did it. One reason for this is because this mundane task simply wasn't important enough to give you that feeling of success. Other examples of similarly unexciting everyday tasks include putting on your shoes, washing your face, locking your door, taking out the trash, or charging your phone. This is also true in our working lives. When it comes to the work we do, we cannot feel successful if we don't feel like what we are doing is important to us. And because the feeling of importance often comes from having a sense of purpose, this makes purpose a common characteristic of people who feel successful.

The path to success is often long and, frankly, quite painful. If you look at the life stories of many people who feel successful, you'll find lots of hard work and struggle, especially in the beginning of their journey. In many cases, they didn't feel like a success for many years, but endured lots of difficult experiences during that time that would make most people quit. Why does becoming successful require so much pain and struggle? Although success is a creation of our minds, the mind is picky about when it grants the feeling. Just how picky depends on the individual, but everyone's mind, including yours, insists on having at least some amount of struggle. However, it won't tell you this directly. Instead, it will choose to reward you with a successful feeling only for things that are difficult. To be clear, it doesn't mean you dislike what you're doing, it just means it isn't easy—the two concepts should never be confused with each other. If you do a great job of checking your mailbox, washing your face, or charging your phone, these accomplishments still won't give you that feeling of success in part because they are just too easy. This is because the effort we put into something is often related to the value we place on it.[3] Mountain climbers and ultra-marathon runners value what they do in part because it requires a tremendous amount of effort.[4] Even the food we eat can taste better if we make it ourselves instead of having it prepared by someone else.[5] Similarly, the effort required from us is part of the formula our mind uses to grant the feeling of success.

Purpose as a Source of Emotional Fuel

When struggling on the road to success, purpose serves as a critical source of emotional fuel to help us move forward. Emotional fuel is the energy that powers us to accomplish our goals, and is one of the most precious resources we have. Positive experiences, including receiving encouragement and support from others, increase the amount of fuel we have and fill our tank, while negative, discouraging experiences can drain our fuel. The path to success often begins as a lonely journey, and the challenges along the way often result in very real feelings of anxiety and emotional pain. The fear of experiencing these negative emotions is one reason why more people don't aspire to be more successful. Many also fear the pain and shame that come with failure. While failure is a product of our own minds, the feelings of pain and shame that come with it are just as real as the joy one feels with success. Experiencing failure on its own is painful, but shame magnifies the experience because it adds a level of negative judgment that directly attacks our self-worth. These fears can be understandably paralyzing.

In order for anyone to become successful, enough emotional fuel is needed to continue moving forward through each of these experiences until they reach the final destination. Everyone will start out thinking they have enough, but events and circumstances happen along the way that no one could have expected. These situations can drain large amounts of our emotional fuel; sometimes we run out before we reach our intended destination, and if we can't find a source to get more we are unable to continue. It's like driving on a desert highway with your fuel gauge warning light on, when the next fuel station is at least an hour's drive ahead. You know at some point soon your car cannot go any further, and you will have to somehow find fuel. If you don't find it soon, the sun will eventually go down and the desert will become much colder and darker, and even seeing the way forward will become difficult. You're still nowhere near your destination though, and without more fuel you can't get there. All of this can make life seem cruel, and perhaps at times it is. But humans actually have an amazing capacity to find emotional fuel, even when we might otherwise feel exhausted and discouraged.

The situation where one is about to run out of emotional fuel is a critical defining moment. It's like the moment described earlier when you're driving a car and the fuel gauge light is on. You may choose to give up and stop, or choose to continue and move forward. But continuing still requires more fuel, which has to come from somewhere. In this moment, a part of your mind will ask a pressing question: *Why are you doing this?* You've answered this question before, but this part of your mind has come back to ask again because it now has doubts. Answering this question again is important, because this part of your mind serves to make sure you aren't wasting precious time and energy. It does not work to simply ignore it, because if you do its voice will only get louder and interfere with your ability to perform. Instead, it needs to be given a satisfying answer. And the answer you give will have a profound effect on what happens next.

If you ask enough people about why they do their jobs, you will hear an assortment of responses from the depressing to the inspiring. Some people do their job because they need a way to survive to meet the basic needs of food and shelter, and maybe have enough for a decent vacation every once in a while. Others do their jobs because they feel strongly that what they're doing is changing the world for the better. And of course, there are many answers in between. What all of these responses have in common is that they provide each person the emotional fuel they need to continue. But these answers don't offer the same amount of fuel. The person who only works to receive their pension in ten years has much less fuel to power them compared to the person who works to save lives every single day. This is obvious if you look at their behavior while engaged in their work. One can't help but bring less energy into their work because the fuel isn't there, and the other will seem to have almost limitless energy, constrained only by what their body will physically tolerate. In order to achieve success then, one needs to have an answer to "Why are you doing this?" that provides as much fuel as possible. And a strong sense of purpose offers the best answer one can have to give them that fuel. It should be no surprise then, that many genuinely successful people in this world have a strong sense of purpose—it provides the foundation necessary in order to feel successful, and the most fuel to finish the drive along the road to achieving success.

3

THE CHALLENGE OF PIVOTAL LIFE DECISIONS

The only thing that makes life possible is permanent,
intolerable uncertainty; not knowing what comes next.
~ Ursula K. Le Guin

Every narrative worth telling about a person's life has three elements:

- the person's circumstances
- their decisions
- the outcomes of their decisions

If the narrative covers a long-enough period of time, there will be a moment where a pivotal decision must be made that will change the course of their entire life path. This is a feature of how life itself works. The older you get, when you look back on your life up to the present, you realize it was just a few decisions at critical moments in your past that explain most of why your life is the way it is now. Maybe it was moving to a new place far from home, where you met the person you'd eventually marry. Maybe it was accepting that job offer to finally take on an important management role, which led to getting noticed by the right people. Or, maybe it was turning down that same job offer, because you believed where you were already was the best place to be. If purpose is the bridge between the external world and our true self, how well we build and strengthen the bridge depends to a large extent on the decisions we make in these pivotal moments.

The Three Tools

How is one supposed to reach a decision in these circumstances? As humans, we all have the same set of tools to help us: rational logic, intuition, and emotion.

Rational logic usually boils down to some kind of weighing of pros and cons, and requires making assumptions about what will happen in the future. It's the easiest method to explain and justify to others, which makes it a favorite for those who need validation from others that they are making a good decision. Especially for those who work in large organizations, an overwhelming bias exists to make decisions this way because it's easier to convince others your decision is correct and that you are a diligent and thoughtful contributor. A sense of satisfaction also comes with this approach from exerting all the mental effort to do the analysis, which makes you more confident your choice must be the right one because of all the work you did, or at least the best anyone could do under the circumstances.

Unlike rational logic, intuition is the sense of knowing something instinctively without the need for any kind of conscious reasoning. It's that feeling you get when you meet someone everybody loves but you somehow feel like they can't be trusted. Or, when you meet your friend's fiancé, and have a bad feeling the marriage won't last but can't point to any clear reason why. We don't teach intuition in school mostly because we have no idea how to, and it's hard to get a degree in something you can't analyze and break down into understandable pieces. But make no mistake, intuition is real, and many of the world's most successful people rely heavily on their intuition to do the extraordinary things they do.[6] Intuition isn't the word they use to describe their process, though. They will usually say they just went with their gut feeling.

Emotions are easier for us to understand because even at a relatively young age we have already experienced all of them. They include physiological states you feel through your body, and can be thought of as signals about the situation you're facing. If you're walking alone in a dark alley at night, you may feel something you understand to be fear. If you joke around with your best friend, you may feel something you understand to be joy. If you're at a party and run into someone you don't like, you may feel something you understand to be contempt. However, relying on emotions when making decisions is not always straightforward. If you don't feel like getting off the couch and exercising because you feel sad, you probably should ignore that feeling and do it anyway because it's good for you. If you normally feel miserable every day at work, ignoring that signal is a bad idea. Emotions must be clearly understood with a conscious awareness that must be developed, and appropriately managed. However, like intuition, we don't really teach much about this in school.

Limits of the Three Tools

For every decision we make in our lives, we use at least one of these three tools—rational logic, intuition, emotion—to help us. However, we're given surprisingly little guidance on when or how exactly to use these tools. For many decisions, this doesn't matter much because the situations have relatively little at stake. For example, if you use your intuition and decide to meet someone for a first date only to discover they aren't a good match, the worst thing that happens is an awkward meeting. But for pivotal life decisions, the stakes are far higher than an uncomfortable meeting with a stranger, and the outcomes have a much more profound effect on our life path. As I mentioned earlier, we don't teach intuition or how to understand emotions in school, so you're already conditioned to be biased to using some kind of rational logic to make your decision. If you did well in school, then you're going to be even more biased in favor of it because it provided you rewards in the past, and if you didn't, you're likely to be more open to listening to your intuition and emotions. Unless of course, you were told to suppress them.

One popular version of using rational logic is quantitative analysis. Numbers have a very reassuring quality about them, where having a model tell you that Choice A pays $100 while Choice B pays only $80 makes it incredibly obvious that Choice A is superior. A classic example in a business setting is analyzing whether buying one type of machine (Machine A) versus another (Machine B) to manufacture a product would be more profitable, assuming everything produced can be sold for a set price. If we know how much each machine costs to buy and operate as well as how many units each machine can produce each day, we can do a straightforward comparison of the profit earned from each one. The machine that produces more profit (assuming it's greater than zero) is what the analysis tells us we should buy. In universities, we teach courses that offer quantitative tools that provide answers just like this, and they work beautifully for solving specific types of problems. But when they are given the task of making pivotal life decisions, they do a terrible job without additional guidance.

Quantitative models work well when one has good data about the range of possible future outcomes, as well as the probabilities of each outcome occurring. But with pivotal life decisions, it's difficult to say with much confidence what the range of possible outcomes is beforehand, and it's not easy to estimate what the probabilities are of each possible outcome occurring. For example, how could you reliably guess who in your new workplace will really support you and who will make your life difficult before even starting there? And more importantly, how much they will support you, or make your life more difficult? There are too many factors like this that are difficult to easily know. If you made the same type of decision many times, there would be more data to improve the accuracy of your model. But everyone has too few pivotal moments in their lives, which isn't nearly enough data. Of course, this doesn't stop some from trying. In graduate school, I knew someone who believed in these models so much that he used them to make all of his major life decisions, including who to marry. As of the time of this writing, he is divorced. I still have no idea where the probability estimates in his model came from.

Even if one doesn't take a quantitative approach, one could still try to apply at least some kind of rational logic in their decision-making process. After all, it's what we professors taught so many of you to do in school. But even then, things usually don't work much better, and for the same reason. If you accept a new job offer, you may know how much you'll be paid in the beginning, your job title, and maybe some details of your benefits package, but it's hard to be sure about much more than that until after you've accepted. At least to some degree, you're leaping into the unknown. You haven't met all of your coworkers, you don't know the unwritten rules, you haven't heard the relevant gossip, and you aren't aware of all the delicate relationships and/or tensions between people at work. You don't have a good sense for what working there really feels like until you've spent some time immersed in it. The limitations of using rational logic to make the big, pivotal, path-changing decisions of our life illustrate a fundamental problem everyone faces when trying to make the right choice. It's very hard to predict what the outcomes are for any possible decision we can make, and there isn't enough data to be that helpful, at least not without some form of additional guidance. Many people might believe they make their pivotal life decisions based primarily on rigorous rational thinking, but because of these limitations this simply isn't true.

Aside from the challenge of predicting outcomes accurately, there is one other significant limitation of using rational logic for pivotal life decisions. It turns out our rational minds are actually not very good at making decisions that produce happier emotional states.[7] Our rational minds are really like computers, which we feed data and run to solve problems. If you have a list of things you need to get done tomorrow, you can ask it to organize them and create a schedule that ensures everything will be done efficiently. It's great at solving these types of problems, and there are lots of well-paying jobs that depend heavily on our rational mind. But the computer part of our brain is often not that well connected to our emotional side. It can struggle to comprehend, let alone analyze, our emotions. I saw this often with my students when they were faced with important career decisions. Their rational minds had done the analysis, but hadn't seriously considered why they should expect to be happier with their chosen option. But you don't have to take my word for it. The world is full of people who made lots of "optimal" life choices and somehow ended up miserable, like my student Adrian, the overachiever. Many of these people work in high-paying careers at places with prestigious names. Long ago, out of curiosity, I once got the idea to ask some of my friends in these jobs how happy they were at work on a ten-point scale, ten being the happiest they could imagine being in any job. The highest number I ever heard was six, and most rated their happiness much lower. I don't ask this question anymore.

If rational logic doesn't work well, then what about intuition or emotion? Both of these can certainly be helpful. When you interviewed with your potential future boss, you may have had a feeling in your gut which made you very comfortable or uneasy. When you met everyone you'd be working with, you may have had clear feelings about who you liked and didn't like, but getting to know them well in that short introduction would have been impossible. Still, all of this is relevant and useful information that should be considered. But it's rarely reliable enough to make pivotal changes in our life path without additional guidance. Like the computer that is our rational mind, intuition and emotion were never meant to carry such a heavy burden, at least not alone. In fact, all three of these tools were meant to support a guiding piece to steer them, a leader we must create first. The leader is our vision—an image of the future we desire, created in our mind.

Our Leader Is Our Vision

Human beings were built to thrive in an uncertain world. At no point in humanity's existence has anyone ever truly known their future beforehand, and certainly not when having to make pivotal life decisions. Despite this, humans have been able to accomplish extraordinary things that have changed our world, and how we think and live. What all these achievements throughout history have in common is an intentional vision that came first, which then led to the actual achievement that came later. No one accidentally built the ancient Pyramids of Giza, the first automobile, or the first ship that took humans into outer space. Visions, whether they be large or small, are how we create certainty in an uncertain world.

How are we supposed to create a vision? At first glance, the task may seem daunting. There isn't an obvious best way to do it, and people create their visions in a variety of ways. What we know is that our society advanced and grew because of people who achieved visions that most people at the time thought were daring, or even foolish. Then, after they achieved their visions, people built statues of them and celebrated their contributions. If you think about it, it's a very odd way for humanity to advance. You'd think we'd all be encouraging each other to push the limits of our imaginations, and trying to find ways to help people fulfill their visions. But if one looks closely, that's not how society operates at all. Instead, we try to limit or diminish the visions of people if they are too bold for our tastes and imagination, and we often do this with the best of intentions. This leads to a mindset that kills creativity, pushes us only to what others will approve of, and encourages us to keep our heads bowed in acceptance of the status quo. One has to wonder how much more we would have advanced as a species by now, if only we encouraged each other a little more.

When created the right way, a vision enables a deeper engagement with work that aligns with your true self, by clearly articulating what you intend to do. It's only in the creation of your vision that the question of purpose can begin to be answered in a satisfying way. A well-crafted vision that resonates strongly as right for you is what provides a compelling sense of purpose, a bridge that connects the external world to your true self. It is not the same thing as having a goal, because simply having a goal does not necessarily align with your true self. Many of my students had ambitious goals; very few had well-crafted visions. This may sound heavy, but it's true: Your vision is nothing less than your message to yourself and the world explaining what exactly you are here to do. It provides specific guidance on what decisions you're supposed to make, and defines how you're going to contribute to society. If your contribution changes our lives for the better, you will be celebrated by those whose lives you have touched. The lack of a vision defaults to an existence where one wanders through life following the direction of the wind each day, going nowhere in particular, like a ship adrift in the ocean. Our whole life can go by if we are adrift without ever progressing toward something more fulfilling. Our vision marks a destination that shapes the way forward with our intention, and sets a natural process in motion that begins to respond to it.

When a vision is created, the three tools we've all been given to help us make decisions go to work to make our vision happen. Your rational computer will begin to work out a plan for how you can achieve your vision, given what you already know. In this case, the rational mind is being given a different problem to solve than the one mentioned earlier. The earlier problem might be described as "Which choice is the better one?" while the current problem is "Which choice is the better one to achieve my vision?" If your vision is clear, the second problem is easier for the rational mind to analyze because the problem is much more narrowly defined.

As an example, Cindy was a student of mine who struggled to decide between a job offer from a well-known global bank and a chance to intern for a nonprofit organization focused on improving global health. The offer from the bank included far more money and a clear upward career path if she continued with the job. By contrast, the internship paid only enough to survive and had an unclear career trajectory at the outset. What ultimately helped her decide was remembering that what excited her was the idea of helping others improve the quality of their lives by having better health, which helped her more clearly weigh the costs and benefits of the two options.

The vision you have guides the evaluation process when you make decisions. This doesn't necessarily mean it becomes easy, but it improves the chances rational logic will be helpful, despite its limitations. Also, the rational mind doesn't have to try and assess which choice will make you happier; it only needs to evaluate which one will be better for realizing your vision, which is a better match with its strengths.

With a vision in mind, your intuition will focus on providing critical information your conscious mind cannot, and you will have a sense of knowing in certain key moments that you should or should not be doing something, although you may not know exactly why. Your emotions will serve to tell you whether you're on track, especially if they're sending consistent feelings over a long period of time. At some point, they may even tell you your vision isn't the right one for you. The difference is subtle, but a distinction exists between how setbacks and challenges make us feel and the feeling of disconnection and emptiness with the work itself. Setbacks and challenges drain us emotionally because they are negative experiences of specific events; disconnection and emptiness with the work itself constantly drains us regardless of whether the events we experience are positive or negative. You have to know yourself well enough to tell the difference, but one way to get a better idea of which one you're feeling is to do something that significantly recharges your emotional fuel, like immersing yourself in a very supportive, positive environment away from your daily routine, and seeing how you feel when you return. If the problem was simply that specific events drained your emotional fuel, it should feel good to be back. If it doesn't feel good to be back, examine what might be causing you to feel this way. You're getting a signal something isn't right, and it's possible the vision isn't right for you, even if it seemed like it would be at the outset.

If you're feeling lots of emotions telling you your vision isn't right, don't misinterpret this as failure, even if there are people who would like to tell you otherwise. Visions can be updated as many times as needed and old ones can even be revived, because it is supposed to be a process of iteration. If you look closely at the life stories of most people who became wildly successful, you'll find their first few attempts at achieving their visions never quite ended up working out. This is easy to forget, because everyone is so busy celebrating their successes.

One example of this iterative process is the experience of Walt

Disney. While Disney is recognized as one of history's most successful creative entrepreneurs, his path to success was filled with numerous struggles. Disney's first animation studio went bankrupt after just two years, which led him to move to Los Angeles to try and get a job as a director at a movie studio. Unable to find a job as a director, he then tried again to build another animation studio. Finally, he got his first taste of success when he created the character Oswald the Lucky Rabbit, whose cartoons were purchased by Universal Pictures. However, the joy was short-lived; almost all of his animators abandoned him to work for his producer, and he lost all legal rights to the cartoon character he had created. Feeling angry and betrayed, it was soon after this experience that he would create the character Mickey Mouse, which we're all familiar with today. But the challenges didn't end there. He would be rejected over 300 times by banks before one would finally agree to give him the financing needed to make his first Mickey Mouse cartoon.[8] The story of Disney's success is one of remarkable perseverance through a long series of painful setbacks, but most of us don't think of him in this way. We simply recognize the extraordinary contributions he made, the outcome of his struggles.[9]

Following Another Leader

By now, you might be thinking everything I've described is far more complicated and involved than how most people make their pivotal life decisions. And you'd be right. Most people don't really follow the process I've described here, or they stop far short of what's needed. Instead, what they do is take a big shortcut that skips much of the self-reflection and personal development required to create a vision that gives a strong sense of purpose. This approach very rarely connects the external world to our true self, and can easily lead to the pursuit of goals that fails to bring the happiness we wanted. After getting to know many of my students over the years from all ages and backgrounds, I witnessed the same pattern over and over again. In everyone's life when pivotal life decisions present themselves, there is a genuine opportunity to tune out the voices from the outside world and look within. It's a moment where we can ensure our vision is well-crafted and authentically aligns with our true self. That's how it's supposed to be done if we want to look back on our life later and feel like we've done what we were meant to be doing. But in that same moment, the external world also offers a shortcut. And that shortcut is to do what someone else tells us to do, and serve their interests instead.

4

SOCIETY WASN'T (EXACTLY) DESIGNED FOR YOUR HAPPINESS

Society attacks early, when the individual is helpless.
~ B.F. Skinner

If having a strong sense of purpose with our work can significantly improve the quality of our lives and help us be successful, it seems obvious we would all be better off if we had it. And yet, many people in the world go to work every day without it. One reason this happens is the society we live in doesn't really care if we feel purpose or not, even if we do. This on its own wouldn't be a problem, except that our society isn't neutral about what path we choose, either. While we all have the capacity to create a vision for our life and begin working toward it, we also learn the external world prefers we choose some paths over others. These preferences are expressed in countless subtle messages and signs we are constantly exposed to, which we often absorb without being fully conscious of what's happening. But our society isn't intentionally trying to hurt us; it's simply following its design, created by those who came before us.

Every society is structured according to a deliberate design, which its members generally take for granted as the reality of how the world works. The design dictates what is desired of all of its members in many or all aspects of life, and offers corresponding benefits for everyone who delivers. For example, in principle an employee who contributes significantly to accomplishing their employer's goals may be continuously promoted and eventually join senior management. As they continue to be promoted, they can usually expect to receive greater monetary compensation. Multiple institutions are also created, like schools and a code of laws, which work to create productive members who will contribute to society in the way it desires. It would be nice to think our society is designed to help us maximize our potential as human beings, and to encourage us to have purpose and feel successful. But instinctively you already know this isn't true. So, what is our society designed to do, exactly? It's not as difficult to find out as one might think. To understand what a society is designed for, one only has to look at what its most important measure of progress is. Since the mid-20th century, that measure has predominantly been Gross Domestic Product (GDP) for almost all countries on Earth.

Progress = GDP

If you don't remember exactly what GDP is from your high school economics class, don't feel too guilty. One feature of our society's design is that its members don't need to understand what measure of societal progress they're contributing to; they simply need to comply with the various messages and nudges given to them over their lifetime. Gross Domestic Product is the market value of all the goods and services produced in a specific time period. The measure is most often used for countries, and because population sizes differ greatly across countries it's usually divided by the total population, which gives the GDP per capita. If economics wasn't your favorite subject in school or if you never studied it, don't worry, there's no need to overthink this. Think of GDP as a measure of economic output, and you've got the idea. That's generally how everyone has been measuring societal progress for decades.

If you're uncomfortable with the idea of using GDP as our primary measure of societal progress, you're not alone. Even the economist who invented the measure, Simon Kuznets, didn't like how it came to be used. He knew society was much more complex than what could be captured by his measure, and he also knew relying on it too much would oversimplify issues that should be considered much more thoughtfully.[10] But it became the de facto standard for societies around the world anyway. And because we've used it this long, it has profoundly shaped our society and our lives, mostly in ways we aren't consciously aware of.

What exactly is wrong with using GDP? It has many limitations, but a glaring one is that it doesn't capture many aspects of what we would consider important for our quality of life. For example, consider mental health. A society focused solely on GDP might create work environments where producing more goods and services is so important that it forces employees to work long hours under constant stress and anxiety, which they then bring home to their families at the end of every workday. The stress and anxiety they bring may then have a negative effect on the mental health of everyone else in the household, including children. As a way to remain functional and productive they may pay to see a psychiatrist, who will then encourage them to buy antidepressant medications. Ironically, this would actually be good for GDP. All of this will look like societal progress, and economists at the government bureaus who track the numbers will declare everything is progressing nicely in our world. But is it?

To be fair, one could do much worse than choosing GDP as a measure. Countries with higher GDP generally have fewer people who live in economic poverty, more people who earn high-enough incomes that allow for a wide range of leisure activities, and more resources to provide social services to their populations. So, using GDP as a measure does capture some aspects of what we might consider to be a good quality of life, especially when it comes to meeting some of our most basic needs. But its failure to capture others, such as mental health, means there are also things that are left out, creating a misalignment between our needs as humans and the design of our society. It turns out our society wasn't exactly designed for our happiness, at least not beyond a certain point.

If GDP is so obviously flawed as a measure of societal progress, why did almost everyone in the world choose it? One reason is, GDP made a lot more sense to use at the time it was first adopted. In the mid-twentieth century, humanity had finished one of its darkest chapters with the end of World War II. Roughly three percent of all humans on Earth died as a consequence of the war, and many of the factories and businesses that would otherwise have allowed people to earn income for food and shelter were destroyed.[11] There was an urgent need to help much of humanity meet its most basic needs. There was also a realization that one of the causes of the war was economic instability. With this in mind, leaders of the allied nations gathered in Bretton Woods, New Hampshire in 1944 to reach an agreement on how to improve political stability and foster peace through international trade. Their idea was that by encouraging international trade, the resulting economic growth would create jobs and improve the quality of people's lives. This would lead to political stability, and hopefully a lasting peace between nations. The meeting at Bretton Woods planted the seed that would eventually grow into the popular belief that economic growth was equivalent to societal progress.[12] Finding purpose and meaningful work would have to wait until another day.

GDP was also chosen because it's a simple, numerical measure. Taking really complicated things and making them easy to use is something humans spend a lot of time and effort doing. It really works well a lot of the time, especially when we build machines. We don't need to understand much to effectively use our smartphones, but if you look inside your phone you'll see a complicated device with hundreds of parts working together to let you connect with the rest of the world. It's tempting to think we can apply the same approach to designing our society as well. Imagine you're in a meeting of government bureaucrats where everyone in the room has to decide what the best measure of societal progress should be for the country. The presenter standing at the front of the room is arguing for GDP, a single measure that covers a lot of people's basic needs and can be quantified reasonably well. Their presentation is easy to follow and understand, so you know it won't be hard to explain and sell to others in the government. Also, depending on your point of view, you may not even believe humans have any other needs beyond what GDP captures, or that government should pay attention to them. Then, the next presenter walks to the front of the room and proposes a much more complicated measure of societal progress that includes fuzzy things like happiness, which is much harder to quantify. Their presentation is hard to follow because so many more pieces are introduced, only one of which is GDP, and you can clearly see it wouldn't be easy to explain to others, let alone convince them to use it. The meeting drags on and everyone grows tired, but a decision must be made. It's not difficult to imagine how GDP could emerge as the winner.

A Society Shaped by GDP

When a society has chosen its measure of progress, it grows into something much more significant. It actually defines a society's culture. It defines what is valued, and by default what is not valued. By declaring the measure of societal progress to be GDP, this influences everything else in our society to be structured to support GDP growth. We need companies that perpetually grow, and the faster they grow the better. We need people to be even more productive than the year before. When governments debate about whether to regulate an industry due to the environmental damage it creates, the consideration of costs to the country's GDP is often powerful enough to stop any serious action. The leaders of the best-performing companies appear on the covers of magazines, and we celebrate them as examples others should envy and follow. They have unquestionably helped increase GDP, as we all should.

If one dominant measure is used to gauge the advancement of society, then society will naturally do everything it can to improve that measure, often at the expense of everything else. And that improves the quality of our lives, to a degree. But beyond a certain point, it actually begins to hurt us. As I mentioned earlier, our society sends messages and gives nudges to all of us as part of its design, to encourage us to comply with what it wants. It isn't true that having a strong sense of purpose at work is at odds with increasing GDP, so it might seem that purpose could be encouraged as part of our society's design, and it certainly is possible. But our society is structured to grow GDP in the most direct and predictable way, and the most straightforward design is one that allocates its members as efficiently as possible based on only a surface judgment of their value. Purpose is pushed into a cold and distant corner of attention, if not completely ignored. In order to better understand how this happens, there are two parts of our society we need to examine more closely: one is our schools, and the other is the employers we work for.

Earlier, I mentioned that virtually every country on Earth in the twentieth century embraced GDP as their primary measure of progress. There was one notable exception—the country of Bhutan. In 1972, the King of Bhutan, Jigme Singye Wangchuck, had serious doubts that using GDP alone would lead to a happier, more developed society. As an alternative, he proposed the idea of Gross National Happiness (GNH), which he felt should take priority over GDP.[13] The measure that was eventually created aimed to capture other factors such as psychological well-being, good governance, and protection of the natural environment. More recently, other countries are increasingly considering the adoption of similar types of measures of societal progress, as opposed to relying solely on GDP. Only a teenager at the time in 1972, King Wangchuk of Bhutan deserves credit for recognizing the problem and working toward an alternative. He was decades ahead of the rest of us.

5

OUR EDUCATION SYSTEM: BUREAUCRACIES IN NEED OF REFORM

It is . . . society which, according to its particular structure, shapes education in relation to the ends and interests of those who control the power in that society.
~ Paulo Freire

To understand why our education system operates the way it does today, we first need to consider how it evolved over time. The idea that everyone in society should receive formal schooling is a very recent concept in human history, one that emerged during the last several hundred years. In fact, if providing formal education for everyone was always part of humanity's destiny, one could argue we weren't in much of a hurry to accomplish it. For thousands of years, formal schooling was generally only available for a privileged few who were members of the elite social classes within society. The majority of humans on Earth never attended school, and remained illiterate throughout their entire lives.[14] Because of their inability to read, written knowledge passed from one generation to the next was inaccessible, crippling their capacity to learn. This is not because we were incapable of providing education at a larger scale until recently. An education system is a necessary feature of every society, and every society creates one. But the question of who should receive it, and how much they should receive, depended upon the perceived need for it.

Education systems throughout the world were constructed primarily to satisfy the needs of groups within each society, not of the individual receiving the education. There is a certain cold logic to this. Educating humans requires an enormous amount of time and effort, often demanding customized individual attention to be effective. If someone is going to make the investment, doing so is much easier if a compelling argument can be made for how it serves their interest. Throughout most of human history, much of the work societies needed to be done was often physically demanding but required little or no formal schooling. In order to meet these needs, our ancestors who designed these societies created institutions to provide large and stable supplies of cheap labor. A straightforward way of ensuring an abundant supply of labor was to define groups of individuals within society whose rights and freedoms would be severely restricted, effectively forcing them to do the required work in order for everyone to survive, and for those in charge to prosper. These institutions included slavery and indentured servitude, which directly addressed the problem of finding cheap labor.[15] They allowed societies to flourish according to their design, but also led to a significant percentage of humanity having neither the freedom nor resources to explore their own interests. By structuring societies in this way, there was little obvious reason to provide education to everyone, and only a small percentage of society's members were perceived as needing a significant amount of it. Compared to the world we live in today, our ancestors had a particularly dim view of human beings and their potential.

Roughly 150 years ago, and especially after World War II, things began to change drastically. Mandatory schooling for everyone in society became the accepted norm throughout the world.[16] The average number of years individuals spent in school increased, and a much higher percentage of individuals continued their education after high school. Machines also became more efficient than humans in doing a growing number of tasks, especially in manufacturing products. Increased automation meant that human labor was no longer cost-effective to do certain jobs, but new jobs were created that needed different types of skills. Many of these new jobs were less physically demanding but much more cognitively demanding, and required significant formal schooling. Education systems helped fuel economic growth throughout the world by producing a skilled supply of labor, bringing increased prosperity.

Most of humanity also experienced an extraordinary transformation in their quality of life. In 1820, roughly three-fourths of the world's population was living in extreme poverty, but almost 100 years later, by 2018, that fraction had fallen to one-tenth, with the most rapid decline occurring in the last several decades.[17] Slavery and indentured servitude were also abolished across many countries. Those previously too poor and destitute to consider much more than their daily survival became used to having their basic needs easily satisfied. Now, in the early twenty-first century, an unprecedented number of people on Earth have the freedom and economic means to pursue their interests. The opportunity for humans to craft and achieve their visions has never been better. But our education system has not yet adapted to handle a world with this much freedom.

One primary objective of our current education system is to provide individuals with a core set of skills and knowledge so they may contribute more productively to society. At the high school level, a standard curriculum covers a range of subjects that include math, literature, science, and history, which is often extended further in postsecondary education along with courses required for one's major. The system provides employers with a supply of skilled labor, qualified candidates they can hire to work in their organizations. The system also allows for, in theory, a better-functioning government, since having better-educated citizens may lead to the adoption of better policies. There is nothing wrong with having an education system that serves this objective—the current system has played a vital role in achieving humanity's recent economic success. But for all the time and effort invested in teaching students subject matter knowledge, remarkably little effort is spent on helping them decide what they would like to do for their working lives. It is an astonishing failure to recognize students as individuals, each with their own need for purpose. While our current system reflects a much more evolved view of human potential than our ancestors who implemented slavery had, it still falls short of acknowledging students as being on an individual journey, where finding purpose is essential to becoming the best version of themselves.

The Failures of Educational Bureaucracy

Why are we so focused on subject matter knowledge, but so indifferent about purpose? On the surface, it may appear this unbalanced focus isn't actually true. The mission statements at many educational institutions give the impression that their main focus is helping students find their purpose. But mission statements often reflect only vague aspirations, not reality. The truth is that educational institutions are bureaucracies, and understanding what a bureaucracy actually does can be achieved by looking at three things:

- The incentive structure
- How performance is measured
- The people who work there

A common feature of most educational bureaucracies is that incentives for teachers are incredibly weak. There is little reward for good performance, and little or no penalty for poor performance. The very best-performing teachers in a school are paid similarly to the very worst- performing teachers, and sometimes substantially less if the worst performers have worked for many more years.[18] It's difficult to overstate what having this type of incentive system does to people over time, especially if one encounters too many poor performers as peers. Imagine being a new teacher in a school, in your first year on the job. You bring all the idealism and passion for teaching that your own education inspired. You are ready to change the world. Soon after starting, you notice some of your colleagues don't care about their job performance as much as you do. In fact, some care so little you find their behavior upsetting for your idealistic view of education. They make sure to be vocal and appear engaged when in meetings, but quietly disengage when they think no one is paying attention. You think, surely there must be some consequence for this? And indeed there is, for the teacher's unlucky students.

But as time goes by, you realize no one seems to have a problem with what's going on except you. If you begin to see that many of your colleagues are this way, it becomes increasingly difficult to explain to yourself why you continue to work longer hours and emotionally invest more in your students. You may start to wonder if your life would be happier if you simply stopped trying so hard. It certainly would be easier. As much as we'd all like to think our motivation and behavior isn't affected by our environment, the truth is that for even the most independent and stubborn among us, our environment often influences how we feel and what we do. Incentives, or the lack of them, are a powerful force that shape how bureaucracies operate. To the extent teachers are given incentives, they are overwhelmingly focused on helping their students gain competence in the subject they teach, which is already a tough challenge. It's not hard to see why, given the structure of the bureaucracy, there might be little incentive to help students find their purpose.

Similar to a society's measure of progress, a bureaucracy's choice of performance measure tells you a lot about its design. What gets measured is what gets evaluated, and guides the decisions of its leadership. The choice of measure directly defines the priority in an organization's structure. For primary and secondary education, performance on standardized test scores across various subjects has become a popular measure of teacher and school performance throughout the world.

School administrators may also visit the teacher's classroom and give a personal assessment. However, these measures don't capture anything about how much help students receive in finding purpose. Even the concept of purpose and its importance is nowhere to be found. In higher education, common performance measures include the research productivity of faculty, graduation rates, and job placement rates. Among these measures, the most relevant to a student's search for purpose is job placement rates. But finding purpose requires much more exploration and self-reflection than simply finding a job. Similar to primary and secondary education, performance measures related to helping students find purpose are noticeably absent in higher education. Instead, our current education system uses measures that only focus on skills and getting a job. One can guess what the consequence of this narrow definition of performance in education might be. Graduates may have skills and be competent at their jobs, but also lack a sense of purpose in their work. Because the cause is systemic, the phenomenon may be so prevalent it is simply considered normal, perhaps even acceptable. And this occurs, in part, because of the way we've designed the bureaucracy.

In spite of all this, even if a bureaucracy's incentives or performance measures don't value something that is desired, it's still possible to see it valued in practice. Whether this occurs depends entirely upon the choices of the people who work inside it. The values and behaviors of leadership in particular matter tremendously in shaping the behavior of everyone in the organization, even when the incentives and measures aren't there. In education, we often hear stories of individuals doing remarkable things, perhaps far more often than one might rationally expect given the bureaucracy's incentives. There are school principals who don't think twice about driving the school buses themselves when drivers can't be found, never uttering a word of complaint. There are teachers who work after hours to give extra help and encouragement to the shy, self-doubting, those with problems at home, and other students who struggle. They make the conscious decision to act according to what education is supposed to be, not what they are incentivized to do. These are extraordinary people, without a doubt. They are often the same people who help students find their purpose. But the far more common story is one of teachers losing morale and motivation, and growing numb to the failures of the bureaucracy they're a part of. This happens because the structure of a bureaucracy is often too powerful a force to ignore, and because good leadership is too rare to be relied upon to compensate for its weaknesses. On its best days, our education system fails to recognize the efforts of teachers in helping students find their purpose, and on its worst days, it punishes them for paying too much attention to what is not measured for performance.

Where Purpose Dies

In my early years as a professor, I discovered one reason why I had so many students coming to my office to ask for advice about their careers: they felt like they had nowhere else to go. I later found this wasn't an issue specific to any individual school, but was a much broader phenomenon throughout our higher education system. My students had made their initial career choices not based on serious self-reflection, but by selecting from a limited menu that was handed to them by the institution and the employers who visited campus. What was supposed to be an initial limitless personal reflection and exploration exercise was instead a task of picking the best option on an artificial list. Creativity, imagination, and true self-awareness were skipped entirely in the process.

Where our education system failed to help my students in finding their purpose, other voices confidently gave their own guidance. Some of my undergraduate students chose their major because their parents had forbidden them from following other paths. The heavy-handed direction they received was always well-intentioned, but my students often felt trapped if their emotions clearly warned them that the path dictated to them was the wrong one. Their parents had grown up with a different reality, and couldn't see that the world offered their children much more freedom and opportunity than they could imagine. When I later taught older students, I realized one did not outgrow the feeling of being trapped if they stayed on the same path their parents desired. Instead, the feeling would continue to grow, as if one had entered a prison cell but spent years to figure out that it was, in fact, a prison they had entered of their own choosing. Once the realization settled in, by the time they came to my office they could see where they had always wanted to go—far off in the distance from the window of their cell—and wondered how they ended up spending so long traveling down the wrong road.

If their parents had not forced a direction, the pressure to find a job would often fill the void. All of my students knew they needed to get a job upon graduation, otherwise they would experience some very unpleasant blows to their self-esteem. Not getting a job would mean they had failed, weren't good enough, were supremely unlucky, or would be labeled as otherwise damaged. This pressure was multiplied many times over by comparing themselves with their classmates, some of whom had found attractive-sounding job offers quickly and were breathing joyous sighs of relief. For many of my students, the process of getting a job felt like being in a race, and not a time of self-reflection and appreciation for one's own vision.

With this much pressure weighing on them, my students weren't nudged that hard to make their choices, and they didn't need to be. Employers coming to campus did a good job of selling themselves as great places to work, full of opportunity. Some had prestigious reputations which implicitly signaled that working there would be a validation of my students' abilities and worth, similar to getting good grades in the educational bureaucracy. By having a pool of interested applicants that was larger than the number of available positions, the competitive structure for getting a job was often enough on its own to drive many of my students to view getting a job as a game they needed to win. Whether they won or lost, at least trying to win a game was much more straightforward than exploring the deeper question of what they really wanted out of life. And if it was a game, then being handed a limited menu of choices made the process that much easier. It clarified the meaning of winning and losing, and conveniently let them ignore the fact that their lives were never supposed to be based on an artificial competition created by others.[19]

For my students, the education they received throughout their lives never taught them that purpose was something they needed to pay attention to, let alone value. In a system where almost no effort had been made to explore what might genuinely align with them as individuals, I tried to help those who visited my office in the short time we spent together. But it is hard to fight a system, and the undeniably powerful pressures these students often faced from others and the race to find employment. All too predictably, I would later hear from my students years after graduation, and learn that many of them disliked their jobs.

6

EMPLOYERS: NO PLACE FOR PERSONAL REFLECTION

Even in a crowd, you are alone inside your own head.
~ Anonymous

If our education system does little to help individuals find a sense of purpose at work, employers are much more intentional in dealing with the question of purpose. For some employers, a big part of their attraction is offering a chance to engage in work that naturally provides purpose. For example, a nonprofit organization with a humanitarian mission may provide free medical treatment to heal those who are sick and have no access to care; one doesn't have to wonder what the point of doing this kind of work might be. For these types of employers, the challenge is not meeting one's need for purpose, but maintaining a strong sense of it in the individuals who have already joined. However, most employers don't offer a strong enough sense of purpose in their mission. And for these organizations, the need for purpose is often handled by different means.

With few exceptions, employers are structured in a way that cannot provide space for the self-discovery needed to find purpose. If my students with full-time jobs needed to reflect on their challenges with work, one reason they visited my office was because their work environments had no safe place to do it. This lack of space is demonstrated across multiple aspects of an individual's employment experience and begins when they first engage in the hiring process, especially for students close to graduation. Growing up in an education system that doesn't help students find purpose, it's only by a remarkable stroke of luck or an extraordinary level of self-awareness that a student arrives adequately prepared to evaluate employers by the time they are interviewing. Many employers recognize this implicitly during their interviews and evaluations by avoiding questions about a candidate's beliefs about their purpose, and instead focusing on assessing skills and personality traits. This leads to a recruitment process that largely, if not entirely, ignores the question of purpose or whether the employer is able to meet the candidate's need for it. It's the giant elephant in the room that must be ignored, because neither side has good news to share. Students have rarely done the amount of self-reflection required to assess their own need for purpose, and so are unprepared in answering this for themselves. I personally saw this countless times in my office. And most employers would rather not admit the truth about how they address the need for purpose: that they hope you will somehow naturally find it while working for them. And if you don't? They discourage you from, if you wouldn't mind, thinking too much about it.

After an individual is hired by an employer, the work environment they enter dictates expectations of their behavior, almost all of which is unwritten and only rarely mentioned out loud. There might be expectations of how many hours one is expected to be in the office, regardless of how much work they have. In meetings, junior employees may be expected to openly give their opinions, or remain silent unless spoken to. There can be significant differences across employers in the definition of acceptable and unacceptable behavior. However, a common trait across many work environments is that speaking openly about one's emotional challenges with their work is discouraged, especially to supervisors. This applies to conversations about purpose, but also reflects a broader suppression of honest dialogue that limits the conversations one can safely have while at work.

The Danger of Honesty at Work

The inability to engage in completely honest dialogue is a central feature of almost all employers. Have a problem with your supervisor? Telling them about it might be risky, because they might conclude you are the problem. Is the person you were assigned to work with not doing their part? It's often easier to compensate by taking on their work instead of raising a formal complaint. This predicament is the consequence of both the hierarchical structure most organizations have and human responses to weaknesses in the structure.

In organizational hierarchies, every individual is part of a chain of command ultimately guided by leadership at the top, which by design creates a bias against reporting any information that may make an employee seem anything other than excited and fully engaged in their work. It's easy for leaders to listen to those who tell them how great everything is, but hard to hear those who bring bad news or ego-bruising criticism. When feeling threatened, the ego will naturally want to label these individuals as poor performers to protect itself. Good managers can separate constructive criticism from signs of poor performance, but it's usually too risky for an individual to test how good their manager truly is. And while many organizations implement ways to mitigate this problem, they are generally intended to solicit feedback that is specific to work activities or actions that directly affect the employee's productivity, and not about how the employee feels more fundamentally about their work. This has the functional benefit of setting the expectation that these types of personal issues should be handled outside the workplace, and establishing a clear focus on getting the work done. However, for the individual who feels a growing sense of emptiness from lack of purpose and needs to better understand the cause of their emotions, this becomes an unhelpful obstacle in their search for a solution. When employers eventually notice the diminished enthusiasm and engagement that comes from this emptiness, it's sometimes framed as a mental health issue. That's one way to look at it. Or maybe it's a perfectly normal reaction when one realizes they aren't living a purposeful life, but cannot talk about it.

Organizational hierarchies don't necessarily have to be places where communication must be so guarded. The leadership in an organization can create a safe place for open and honest dialogue, but whether this occurs depends upon their values and character. In some of my classes a few students would mention instances where they were able to be authentic and open with their supervisors. These students had been fortunate to have a relationship based on trust and mutual respect with those they worked for, sometimes to the point where their supervisors would even help them find their next job elsewhere. But as I've mentioned before, good leadership is rare, and cannot be counted on to exist in one's work environment. For the vast majority of my students, their work environments were never safe places to express their true emotions about work if there were any negative feelings. Although leaders in their organizations would sometimes claim their door was always open to hear concerns, my students understood the reality was different. For a brave few, it was by taking their leaders at their word, only to learn a painful lesson later about the price of honesty in their work environment.

As just one example, Lily was a former undergraduate student of mine who took a job at a consulting firm that publicly stated their monthly town hall meetings were safe places where anyone could freely suggest anything they felt would help the company. Trusting their word, Lily believed them and suggested that increasing the compensation offered to potential new hires to match their competitors might increase their success in attracting talent. The suggestion did not go over well; she was eventually told to resign within five weeks or be fired. Most of my students were not so bold, and learned the same lesson through less dramatic ways, where their first few months at work had given them clear, unspoken messages that open discussion about lacking purpose or other negative emotions was not appreciated.

For the older students who visited my office, the lack of space to engage in the self-reflection needed to find purpose had taken a serious toll. Many looked older than their age, and none could even pretend to have the joy or enthusiasm for life many of my undergraduates had. To my surprise, I also discovered that our meetings were often the first time they had spoken to someone about how they felt. How could it be that along their journey, the first person they felt they could trust enough to speak honestly with was one of their professors? Similar to a patient who had ignored the first signs of a progressive disease, their delay in engaging in self-discovery and adjusting their trajectory compounded what could have been a much smaller dilemma earlier in their life. For years, they had done what was expected of them and in many cases much more, yet they remained unhappy but didn't really understand why. I found that many of them had stumbled into their career paths simply because they accepted, they had thought, the most attractive job offer they had gotten after completing their education. Their first job had made them a logical candidate for their next job, which usually fed into another basket of jobs, and then another basket. They all gave sensible explanations for their choices at every decision point, but somehow their decisions did not address the emotions they brought into my office. And these annoying emotions simply refused to go away.

As I mentioned earlier, not all work environments fail to provide a safe space for self-reflection and questions of purpose. The same way there are extraordinary teachers and principals who ignore the structural failures of their system in order to fulfill the true mission of education, there are managers who unconditionally focus on developing and supporting those around them. They do this because they believe good leadership means developing the people who work for you and seeing them as, ironically, human beings instead of resources to be controlled and manipulated. But similar to our education system, this is not the norm, nor should we expect it to be given how most employers are designed. And if an argument can be made that our education system should help students in finding their purpose, it's less clear whether an employer can be convinced to make the same investment, given the goals of the organization. This is, in part, because there has been a dramatic shift in the employment relationship over the last several decades.

Short-Term Relationships, Little Commitment

For much of the twentieth century in the United States, individuals hired in the private sector could expect to stay with their employers for a remarkably long period of time, if not their entire working lives.[20] The long relationship gave companies the incentive to invest in employees with a very long-term view, and to think of them as lifetime partners. If someone was going to work for a company for life, a high degree of commitment on both sides could also be expected. However, these types of employment relationships began to disappear during the late twentieth century as companies adapted to changes in technology, a greater need to acquire talent with new skills, and increased pressures to produce profits. Other countries experienced similar changes, and the management of employees shifted from having a long-term view to an increasingly short-term focus.[21] Employers with this shorter time frame in mind are more likely to believe they don't have an incentive to help their employees go through the exploration and self-discovery needed to find purpose. However, the lack of long-term commitment from either side also increases opportunities to be hired by other employers, which can be beneficial for those seeking to change their career path. But without conscious effort to counterbalance the constraints placed on them in their work environment and the forces of the external world, individuals can easily find themselves moving forward with no meaningful direction, going from one job to the next.

While the search for purpose is ultimately an individual journey, it doesn't have to be a lonely one. The students who came to my office often felt alone and lost, and I began to understand this wasn't their fault. It was caused by the system we had grown up in, and its failure to acknowledge, let alone provide, what they needed. They had graduated from school and advanced in their careers but received no help from our education system or employers in finding purpose, because neither was designed to constructively address it. They had been given skills to do jobs that were demanded within our society, but they had never been told they had a true self that would not respond well to being ignored. If we genuinely care about the development and well-being of students in education, it's difficult to conclude we haven't left something critical out of the lessons we teach. As for employers, most simply hope their employees naturally find purpose while working for them, so the suppression of open and honest dialogue is one way to deal with the absence of it. If you're in a relationship where the other side doesn't give you something you need, it makes sense that they might try to hide this fact. But employers also present a substitute, which has its own usefulness; they offer the most effective tools in their arsenal to motivate humans, which involve both pleasure and pain.

7

DOPAMINE AND FEAR: HOW MOST EMPLOYERS MOTIVATE US

Nature has placed *mankind under the governance
of two sovereign masters, pain and pleasure.
~ Jeremy Bentham
*(or in modern-day phrasing, "humankind")

In a work environment, how does one get the best from people? Humans have been asking this question for thousands of years, and we continue to struggle with it today. For our ancestors who adopted institutions such as slavery and indentured servitude, the use of physical, often cruel violence was a common answer. One reason why it remained prevalent for so long in our history is because of how easy and straightforward it is; no empathy or real communication skills are required. Good management requires building trust, having the patience to deal with the many needs of those who work for you, and maintaining consistency between what you say and what you do. As any good manager will tell you, the job is far from easy. By engaging in violence, earning trust is unnecessary, undesired behavior has swift and severe consequences, and those who work for you learn to be afraid of you. If one takes this view of management far enough, showing compassion is counterproductive because a sufficient level of fear must be maintained to sustain motivation. Instead, the challenge for management becomes how to keep fear at a high enough level. Some of history's most disturbing chapters demonstrated the creative ways in which our ancestors accomplished this.[22]

By the late nineteenth century, our thinking about how to get the best from people evolved. An American named Frederick Taylor was working as a foreman at a steel factory in Philadelphia, and had become obsessed with increasing the productivity of his workers.[23] In order to understand how much more productive workers at his factory could be, he spent years carrying a stopwatch around the factory floor to measure the amount of time workers took to complete each task in the production process. Then, he ran a series of experiments to see how much faster they were capable of working. His experiments revealed that most were not working nearly as hard as they could, which led to the establishment of clear performance expectations linked to monetary incentives. In his view of the world, workers were productive inputs, which he often compared to oxen or horses, who should be managed with the mindset of an engineer. The productivity increase resulting from his system was extraordinary, and his approach revolutionized how organizations throughout the world were managed, wherever the productivity of humans could be measured and incentivized. This perspective, which considered workers as similar to machines that needed to be optimized as part of a larger system, came to be known as Taylorism.

More recently, other perspectives have emerged to complement Taylorism. It's become popular to tell leaders they need to show empathy, to build trust instead of fear, and to be open and transparent with those who work for them. For those of us who've witnessed or had the experience of dealing with poor leadership, these ideas resonate strongly. It would be nice to think we could do better. But the world we live in today actually reflects a mixed bag that contains the full range of perspectives, including the practice of generating fear. This is because, whether we like to admit it or not, all of these approaches are effective in motivating people to at least some degree, and every manager discovers their strengths and values match best with a unique combination of these perspectives.

Each perspective is ultimately not based on philosophy, but on biology. Our brains are designed to respond to experiences of pleasure and pain, which can help in our survival. If we put our hand too close to a fire, we feel pain and withdraw it to a safe distance. If we eat foods we like, we feel pleasure and consume calories that help power us through the day. Neither works perfectly in always helping us do what's best for us, but these responses are part of how our biology operates at the deepest level. For those who want a very simple explanation for human behavior, one could argue humans live their lives to seek pleasure and avoid pain. And for the pursuit of pleasure, one brain chemical in particular plays a crucial role, which employers and our society more broadly try to induce in a myriad of ways—dopamine.

Dopamine may not be a term you use regularly in your daily

life, but it's a brain chemical you know intimately well from experience. Playing sports, using your smartphone, shopping, cocaine, sugar, and accomplishing ambitious goals can all produce dopamine.[24] Money, or at least the anticipation of receiving it, also produces dopamine and provides the biological foundation for how much of capitalism works.[25] Let's imagine you're about to receive a large sum of money. The sense of want and desire you feel in that moment, that's dopamine. When you receive the money, you might impulsively buy the latest smartphone at a nearby store, which also produces dopamine. Then, feeling hungry, you decide to stop at a nearby fast-food restaurant, which provides plenty of sugar for another round of dopamine. One could argue targeting dopamine is the most straightforward way for a capitalist society to operate, and also aligns well with the measure of societal progress we've adopted because it can easily be used to increase GDP. And employers—especially those unable to meet our need for purpose—use dopamine to motivate us.

Even from a young age, we already understand how employers induce dopamine. Bonuses for good performance, public recognition of one's accomplishments at work, and the potential for being promoted in the hierarchy are all common practices observed across different organizations. And as long as performance evaluations are fair and meritocratic, the system can be effective in getting the best from people. But when I ask my students in class whether they believe they worked in meritocracies, they often give a wide range of answers, with the average being at best a lukewarm positive response. This is, again, partly a challenge of design—true meritocracies are extraordinarily difficult to create in real life. One problem is that for most jobs, measuring everything that defines good performance is incredibly difficult. For example, if we want to reward our managers for coaching and developing those who work for them, how do we measure it? We could ask everyone they supervise to give an evaluation, but there's the risk they might provide subjective responses that reflect workplace politics, unreasonable expectations, or other issues. We could track the number of hours they spend meeting with everyone they supervise as a measure of their commitment, but that's also not a great measure of actual coaching and development. For many organizations, it becomes easier to forego the exercise completely, and instead use subjective evaluations by supervisors in the hierarchy for all employees. However, this exacerbates another problem, which has plagued every organization since the beginning of time.

Ideally, an evaluation of someone's job performance would be unbiased and based on their actual *performance*. While a small number of jobs exist where this is relatively straightforward, such as certain types of sales jobs and for those who trade financial assets, individual performance evaluation is often much more difficult because so much work is done in teams. Although the performance of a whole team might be easy to observe, it's much more difficult to see who contributed more or less of the work that led to the final outcome. This creates two incentives for those who work in teams: 1) to contribute enough to the team to avoid any negative consequence, and 2) to create the impression to those above them in the organization that they are contributing significantly to the team outcome. Someone needs to do the work, but getting credit for it can be an entirely different matter. This can lead one to behave strategically, where one does the bare minimum of work yet creates the appearance they are contributing far more than they are. In smaller organizations this type of strategic behavior is less common because it's much easier to see what everyone is doing. But in large organizations, management's failure to notice these types of behaviors can weaken the effectiveness of monetary incentives because employees lose confidence that the system is a meritocracy. Not surprisingly, when I asked my students if they worked in meritocracies, often the most negative answers I received came from those who worked for large, well-known employers.

If dopamine reinforces the desire for a pleasurable reward, the challenge of creating a true meritocracy can diminish its usefulness in getting the best from people, and may even encourage the wrong behaviors. The effectiveness of using dopamine can also be diminished by other factors, including a lack of trust in leadership, toxic behavior by colleagues, poor communication, and of course, lacking a sense of purpose in one's work. For many of my students who were still in their twenties with decades of work ahead of them, they were already able to share multiple firsthand experiences with each of these issues. Sometimes the dopamine-based incentives still worked, but in many cases, they did little to motivate my students because their work environments were otherwise plagued by too much dysfunction. And yet, none of the organizations they worked for experienced anything serious enough to threaten their survival, no matter how bad things sounded. For the places that were truly dysfunctional and miserable to work at, why didn't everybody just leave? The answer to this usually came from another, perhaps even more powerful force that employers benefit from, one that can be remarkably effective—the fear of an uncertain outside world.[26]

Fear and Being Stuck

For our prehistoric ancestors who were exposed to dangers from their natural environment while hunting and wandering through the wilderness, fear likely played an important role in making sure they stayed safe and avoided unnecessary risk of harm.[27] Fear would have discouraged someone from traveling alone too far from their tribe, where their survival chances would have decreased dramatically. But in the context of the modern working world, this same fear is far less useful, and can do more harm than good. There is no real chance of death, or anything even close to it, when leaving an employer. But for many of us, we fear the pain that may come with leaving what we're familiar with for an unknown world, and the level of fear we create in our minds usually far exceeds the reality of what the future might actually offer us.

One of the most surprising patterns I noticed among many of my students with full-time jobs was how powerful fear was in preventing them from taking action, even when what they needed to do was obvious to them. In many cases, it felt like watching someone starve, yet refuse to search for food. And this was an accurate description of their behavior, at least with respect to their emotional needs. A large part of these conversations consisted of hearing the many reasons why they couldn't leave their employer, then an effort on my part to remind them that it mattered that they were, in fact, miserable, and it was unsustainable to constantly feel this way. The first few times I had these conversations, the situation struck me as bizarre. They had come for advice because they were unhappy but would also make a thoroughly reasoned case that there was nothing they could do about it, leaving me with the task of arguing their emotions demanded a better answer. The walls they had built in their minds to protect them from the outside world were made of fear, which instead trapped them inside a personal hell.

The belief they were stuck in their current job increased the fear of what might happen to them if they somehow lost it. Something too painful to bear might be waiting for them outside, and the uncertainty of what that could be made it even more intimidating. This gave their employers more leverage over them to do as they pleased, and subtle or even unintentional reminders that they could be let go at any time worked to keep their fear alive and well. I began to realize being let go from a job one hated could paradoxically be a blessing for those who were too paralyzed by fear. But even then, this was still not ideal because it reinforced the idea my students were powerless. Of course, they weren't, but their beliefs were in danger of becoming a self-fulfilling prophesy with enough passage of time. As one might expect, I noticed these fears grew much stronger with age, with my oldest students being the most fearful. And as with all fears, the only way to diminish them was to face them directly and not let them define who they were. But battling a beast that only grows with age can be frightening, and the mind can invent more than enough reasons to postpone the battle for a lifetime.

One example was Steven, a student of mine whose job was to trade financial derivatives for a global investment bank. What had initially started as an interesting job that paid well turned into a draining routine that became the bane of his existence. The effect was not only emotional; when he visited my office, he was only in his mid-thirties but looked ten years older. Steven had known for years he needed to make a change, but whenever he saw other opportunities he found more than enough reasons to be afraid of what would happen if he left, which stopped him every time. By the time he came to see me, he only needed one reason to remain stuck: He believed he had gotten too old for the world to offer him anything new.

Different Perspectives of Management Create Our Reality

More recent perspectives on management have evolved from leaning solely on dopamine and fear to motivate us, and are often focused on the brain chemical oxytocin. Like dopamine, oxytocin is also associated with feelings of pleasure, but operates in a very different way. Oxytocin induces a sense of relaxation and increased trust, and plays a vital role in human social bonding.[28] Trust in particular is essential if one wants to get the best from people. However, the lack of it creates an environment where people do not feel safe psychologically, which hurts productivity. That's why every healthy organization has a high level of trust between its members and in its leadership. By contrast, organizations that lack trust must instead rely on dopamine and fear to operate. But how many healthy organizations are actually out there? I was curious myself, so I spent years asking my classes of graduate students this question, and always got the same answer. A few students had discovered their work environments had a high level of trust and psychological safety, and this was always because of their leadership. But for the vast majority, a meaningful level of trust was simply not there. The working world we live in today is dominated by dopamine and fear.

Every employer represents a unique combination of pleasure, pain, and the different perspectives of management mentioned earlier. Each perspective also embodies a clear set of values and beliefs about human beings. That's why different managers will choose a unique combination of each approach, to reflect their own personal values as well as their strengths as a manager. If one believes humans are best motivated by fear, then this will be reflected in how they treat those who work for them. If one believes humans are like machines that must be optimized as part of a larger system, then they will focus on building performance measures and offering monetary incentives. Machines are replaceable if they are not satisfactory, so they may also focus on hiring promising, new people and place less effort on developing those who already work for them. Those adopting more recent ideas of good leadership may work to build trusting relationships with those who work for them, recognizing they are humans with complex emotional needs that matter for their performance. Over a long-enough career, one will encounter evidence of each of these perspectives implemented in practice. However, absent from all of these perspectives is the acknowledgement of an individual's need for purpose.

The Outcome of Our System: Mediocrity

Just how well does our current system, which relies heavily on dopamine and fear, work in getting the best from people? When I began teaching older students, many of whom had already accumulated many years of work experience across different jobs, I wondered just how much of their available energy they put into their work, and how much they saw those around them giving. I asked this question to every class of graduate students I taught, and got a strikingly similar answer over many different groups.

My students claimed that, while it varied depending upon what deadlines they faced, they generally gave only fifty percent of what they had. This wasn't a precise measurement of course, but let's assume it's roughly close to the true answer. Imagine a world where everyone is only giving half of what they can to their work, and multiply that by billions of people. That's this world, today. Then consider how the world might be different if we reshaped our society so people would give fifty-five percent, again multiplied by billions. And what if this increase happened because more of us did work where we felt a stronger sense of purpose? We might see a very different world.

Trading for More Cortisol and Less Oxytocin

The focus on dopamine by employers and more broadly in our society has deeper implications for the quality of our lives because it isn't the only brain chemical that defines how we experience life. The stress we get from work generates cortisol, which was originally intended to deal with the immediate physical threats our ancestors faced. Cortisol is part of the body's fight-or-flight response, which immediately elevates the heart rate, prepares the muscles for a rapid response, and sharpens the brain's ability to assess a threat. These are all helpful, if not lifesaving, for physical threats that only last a short period of time, like a lion chasing you in the wilderness. However, if the stress is constant, which is often the case for work-related stress, cortisol shifts from being helpful to becoming toxic for the body. Too much cortisol production for too long can lead to poor digestion, increases in abdominal fat, decreased immunity, difficulty sleeping, and depression, all of which decrease the quality of life.[29] For many of my students, their career decisions represented a clear trade of increasing cortisol for dopamine. A certain amount of this can be sensible and realistic, but taken too far, the cost of cortisol becomes arguably too high compared to the reward. But many of us aren't even aware we're making this trade, or just how much of our quality of life we're giving away.

Our focus on dopamine also impacts our ability to experience some of the positive effects of oxytocin. Beyond building trust, oxytocin directly reduces cortisol and triggers the opposite of the fight-or-flight response, calming us back down to normal functioning and reducing anxiety.[30] It's a natural antidote we are biologically given to recover from stress and the toxic effects of cortisol. If dopamine can be induced by the anticipation of money, sugar, and smartphone use, oxytocin is instead produced from hugging people, massage, receiving emotional support from others, and petting dogs.[31] But our workplaces usually provide very little space for these types of activities and interactions, and in many instances actively discourage them. Even workplaces that genuinely focus on building trust and exhibiting good leadership face the challenge of providing enough opportunities for oxytocin. If we spend enough hours at work we again make another trade, giving up the chance to produce oxytocin to reduce the effects of stress in exchange for more dopamine.

The imbalance we've created by targeting dopamine, producing cortisol, and limiting opportunities for oxytocin is not a result of nature or an inevitable truth, but a consequence of the way we've designed our society. Focusing on dopamine works to entice and motivate us, but taken to its logical extreme it can easily lower our quality of life. It can lead us down paths with too much chronic stress, declining health, and not enough time spent in social interactions with high levels of trust and genuine care. My younger students interviewing for jobs were largely unaware of the tradeoffs they were making for what they assumed was a better quality of life. My older students came to realize the cost of their choices because their emotions and declining health gave them undeniable signals, but they felt increasingly trapped and powerless to do anything. Was this the best we could do?

One reason capitalism emerged as the dominant economic system in our world is because it's a remarkably effective way to get everyone to organize productively, and both dopamine and fear play important roles in how our system functions. Beyond its link to dopamine, money also plays a crucial role in how our society operates. Money, or at least the promise of receiving it, has had a powerful effect on human behavior since its invention, and throughout history it seems there has always been at least some among us who would be willing to do almost anything for the right price, leaving nothing sacred. Although ideally money should only serve to improve our quality of life, the reality is that humans have had a long and complicated relationship with it, where it's not always clear which side is in control.

8

WHY MONEY WORKS SO WELL, AND WHY IT FAILS SO MISERABLY

Money can't buy happiness, but it can make you awfully comfortable while you're being miserable.
~ Clare Boothe Luce

It's been argued love is the most powerful force that drives human behavior. Stories of the extraordinary sacrifices and risks people take to help those they love are easy to understand because we instinctively know how much influence it has. But if love is the most powerful force, money is not far behind, and at times may even surpass love. Money has led to divorces, caused lifelong conflicts within families, changed the loyalty of many, and led to countless people being killed over the course of history. Of course, money has led to many positive behaviors as well, but the fact that it can motivate such destructive behavior is more telling of the power it holds over us. Money is central to the way our society operates precisely because it's so effective in getting us to do things we might not otherwise do.

The Myth We Want to Believe

Why does money work so well in influencing our behavior? While dopamine is part of the answer, the power money has over us is actually a more complicated fusion of our psychology and the way our society is designed. Society preaches a seductive myth we are all familiar with: money will make us happy and solve all of our problems. While we have all heard at some point that money can't make us happy, these messages are far less frequent and effective than the messages that tell us the exact opposite. Even if we feel unsure about whether the myth is true, we are often willing to pursue money anyway just in case it *might* be true, or at least might be true for *us*. After all, how do we really know money doesn't make us happier unless we receive a lot of it? Some false ideas are so appealing they can only be disproved by pursuing them until reaching a state of personal disillusionment, which must last long enough to leave no doubt in our mind that the idea we believed in was truly wrong from the start.

Our temptation to believe the myth of money leading to happiness doesn't reflect a lack of intelligence so much as a cleverly designed system to target our desire for both happiness and simplicity. The world is infinitely complex, with more data and problems than a human mind can process and solve at any given moment, all of which can easily overwhelm and exhaust us if we let it. In order to deal with our complex world, we need to organize and simplify it so we can accomplish things efficiently. This creates a strong preference to use universal shortcuts and simple rules to solve problems. Our preference for simplicity can be useful for increasing our productivity, but can also get us into trouble when faced with problems that are not easily solved with shortcuts, such as happiness. Biased to choosing a simple answer, the myth that money leads to happiness becomes attractive because it creates a straightforward connection between something we can easily see to something we want to feel. Want to be happier? Get more money. Unhappy again? Get even more money. Not only does this appeal to our desire for a simple universal answer, it's also easy to continue believing it until one actually obtains a large amount of money, because only people who already have a lot of money know with certainty that it is false. The world we live in also, by design, works to perpetuate the myth.

Our society is structured to reward those with money with what, at first glance, appears to be a better life. Having a luxury home, expensive cars, and wearing high-end fashion brands can create the external image of an amazing life, and it's no coincidence many things money can buy are intended to be highly visible to others. These material possessions signal one's status in society, and for those who value moving up in a social status hierarchy, spending money to signal higher status is an important part of improving their quality of life. However, all of these external status benefits would be far less effective if a more honest view was presented of the emotions and thoughts of those who have large sums of money. But this is one of the easiest things for society to hide from us.

A terrible bias exists in what we observe in public and in the media about the emotional well-being of people who have money, which helps to sustain the myth. Formidable pressures and incentives are built into our society to discourage public displays of emotional vulnerability or weakness, which means we usually present an illusion that we're doing better than we actually are. It's much more difficult to see the loneliness, self-doubt, relationship problems, and feelings of emptiness that can also be part of the same life that appears so perfect to the outside world. In fact, when evidence of these negative issues arises, many of us are genuinely surprised. How could someone who has such a great life feel anything close to depression, or even have thoughts of suicide? And for those who have money, an equal surprise is felt when they see the reaction of others: How could anyone truly think money could make a human being happy?

The myth of money leading to happiness also persists in part because there is actually some truth to it. People who have low incomes do tend to be less happy, which is easy to understand.[32] If one is barely able to meet their basic survival needs and has little opportunity to improve their situation, their sense of security, control, and optimism about life is understandably weakened. Both having and earning more money directly addresses this problem. When we struggle to meet our basic needs—having a roof over our heads, a reliable supply of food, clean water, access to medical care, and so on—we focus intensely on doing whatever it takes to survive. Pondering the meaning of life or questions of purpose are luxuries we cannot easily afford. In these cases, receiving more money really can change our lives. All of us understand our basic needs well because we know the consequences of failing to meet them for even a short period of time, and it's easy to imagine how we might feel if we couldn't meet them at all. On the deepest level, we know what this feels like.

By contrast, if our basic needs are met it's much harder for us to predict how much better our lives would be if we received substantially more money. We don't have to stretch our imagination much to know what being unable to eat feels like, but we have to stretch it much further to imagine what a life with more money will feel like if it isn't to meet our basic needs. This is where things can begin to go wrong. We often assume money continues to substantially increase our happiness after our basic needs of food, shelter, and security are covered. When we begin making our most important life decisions based on this false assumption, we risk receiving too little of what would actually make us happier.

The Addictive Hamster Wheel

Money also has another limitation in the way it makes us feel, which ironically makes it even more effective as a motivator. If our basic needs are already met, it offers things and experiences which only make one feel great for short periods of time over the course of their life. Flying first class on an airline, eating gourmet meals, and renting a private island are all fleeting experiences. While a straightforward solution to the brief duration of the high they provide might be to simply continue repeating the experiences indefinitely, the biology of our brains prevents us from receiving exactly the same high again from doing these same things. This creates the need to seek out other ways of getting that great feeling again, and to keep increasing the dosage. If we eat at a restaurant with one Michelin star this week, then next week we may try one with two stars. This may cost more money, so we have a reason to continue working to acquire more. The pursuit of this feeling has no natural ending, and an entire life can be spent seeking enough money to experience more of it. Without sufficient consciousness, this cycle is like a cocaine-addicted hamster running on a wheel, with bloodshot eyes always focused on getting the next high. It's a life where one keeps running with the belief they are making progress, when in reality they continue to be trapped repeating the same loop.

Because money fails to create lasting happiness once our basic needs are met, happiness is often not the right word for what money provides. It's more accurate to say money provides opportunities for pleasure, which is far more fleeting than happiness. While intellectually we can understand this difference, in practice pleasure and happiness are often confused with each other. This is partly because pleasure is much easier to package and sell than happiness, and can appear identical to the unconscious eye. For example, an advertisement for a vacation package can show a person smiling while dining at a beautiful restaurant by the ocean, which is tempting to interpret as happiness. Both happiness and pleasure can cause someone to smile, so it's easy to see the two as the same thing when we see the ad. And if they look the same to us, we might conclude the pursuit of happiness is the same as the pursuit of pleasure.

The Price and Emptiness of Money

There is no question we need money for our basic needs, and there is nothing wrong with using money to obtain pleasure if we understand that's what we're doing. But money is almost never free, and usually costs us in some way. Everything we do for money generally requires we give something else up we value. This trade is part of how life works, but whether we make the right trade determines how we will view our life at the end. Perhaps the most straightforward and important example of this is the time we spend working. If we believe the myth that money leads to happiness, then it makes a lot of sense to spend our life seeking it because pursuing happiness is fundamental to how we operate. If it doesn't work at first, then it's easy to conclude there wasn't enough money acquired and more must be obtained. Then, near the end of our life when looking back, we may feel too many sacrifices were made—and too much time was spent—for things that did not reflect what we really wanted to do with our lives, and for an unnecessary amount of money. But by then, it's far too late to do anything about it.

Money has one other important limitation—on its own, it fails to provide a satisfying sense of purpose. In theory, this seems like it doesn't have to be true. Certainly, there are those who set their primary goal in life as making as much money as possible. Yet even a casual, honest observation of those who work hard only for money across multiple professions reveals money alone doesn't satisfy the need for purpose. I saw this over and over again with my students, but first noticed this long before I became a professor. Part of the reason for this is, beyond meeting our basic needs, money itself lacks much of what would be required to give a true sense of purpose. On its own, it contributes nothing to others or to the world more broadly, so simply possessing it does little outside of one's own existence. This may not seem to be a problem, except it matters tremendously whether we feel we're experiencing life alone or with others, and it's part of our biology to feel this way. Receiving a large sum of money can feel great, but that great feeling always fades if it simply sits in the bank. However, receiving money and then using it to somehow improve how others live multiplies and sustains that feeling. There are many ways one can do this, but there must always be some link between the money and improving how we live in our world. In fact, if one works to acquire money with this in mind, their purpose isn't really the money itself, but the greater goal they aim to achieve. This raises an important defining question, which determines whether we are truly in control of the money, or whether it's the money that controls us: What is the money for? In order to answer this question honestly to ourselves, we must know our own story.

9

THE PROBLEM OF NOT KNOWING YOUR STORY

*If you follow the classical pattern, you are understanding
the routine, the tradition, the shadow
—you are not understanding yourself.*
~ Bruce Lee

Free will is what many believe makes humans different from all other living things on Earth. If true, it's a remarkable gift that gives us the ability to shape the world around us, both for better or worse. Using our own thoughts and intentions, we can build the energy and momentum to create things no one has yet seen. This is not an exaggerated fantasy. The state of our current world and the changes we see happening within it represent the cumulative outcome of everyone who chose to exercise this power. Ultimately, our society is not the product of nature, but of us. As individuals, all of us are here to play some role in all of this. But what is our role?

One of the most challenging conversations I've ever had with a student was with Kate, an undergraduate who came to ask what must have seemed like a perfectly reasonable question in her mind.

"I've noticed that those around me know me better than myself," Kate said. She had come straight to my office from a recruiting event held by a well-known consulting firm, and had swapped the sweaters and jeans she usually wore in class for a crisp, designer-label business suit. "So, now that I'm considering what to do for my career after I graduate, I thought I would come by and ask you. What do you think I should do?"

My students rarely ever told me in advance what they wanted to discuss before they met with me, so I usually had to think on my feet when responding. This time, I found myself dumbfounded.

"You mean, how should you figure out what you want to do for a career?" I replied.

"No, what should I do for my career?"

Both her sincerity and the heaviness of her question felt like the mental equivalent of being sucker punched. I looked at her for a moment stunned, thinking she might either be joking with her professor or that I had misunderstood her question. Neither was true. I didn't want to be dismissive, because she had come to me as someone she trusted. There were not many in her world she could trust for a question like this. But it was also impossible for me to directly answer her. This was the first time we were having a real conversation outside of class, and I had no idea what she should do for a career. I did the best I could to understand who she was as a person, but it was clear a lot more self-reflection was needed to arrive at any helpful answer, and we didn't have enough time. I usually felt good after meeting students in my office, with a sense of accomplishment they had taken one more step in the right direction. But when Kate walked out of my office, I felt we had failed. She graduated soon after our meeting, and I never heard from her again.

It's tempting to think Kate was simply less prepared and, if one takes an uncharitable view, less self-aware than her peers. I don't believe either is true. Other students who visited my office who were highly focused on specific jobs often didn't have any more self-awareness, which I observed repeatedly when I asked why they had chosen their paths. Even though she had surprised me, Kate was simply being honest about what she didn't know, and had chosen the only way she knew how to try to find an answer. Her struggle was entirely understandable. During our meeting, it became clear nothing in her upbringing or environment up until that moment had truly helped her in the search for her own path.

After our meeting, I realized one issue doomed us from the beginning: Kate didn't know her own story. If we all have free will, then we possess the power to create the story of our life. The story of our life is the overarching narrative about why we are here and what we plan to accomplish in a very broad sense. It provides basic principles that guide our choices, in a maze of possible life paths that may otherwise seem completely random. Our story is part of the book being written about our life while it's still unfolding, which includes the trials we face and the outcomes of our choices. We are one author of the book, and the universe is the other. But the universe cannot write anything at all unless we do something first, which makes us the much more important creator. If someone were to read our book, they might learn something about the universe, but what they would really learn is who we are.

The Answer to Why We Are Here

The story of our life is closely related to having a vision, but is much deeper and more fundamental to our identity. It answers the most basic question of *why we exist*. It includes our intentions, but not necessarily how they are expressed or the specific outcomes we hope to achieve. Our story provides the real answer for *why* we do what we do, and the visions we choose provide the answer for *what* we aim to do. Visions can change and be refreshed over the course of our lives, but our story rarely ever does. If we want to have an intentionally created good life, our true self, the story of our life, and our visions all need to be aligned, and cannot be in conflict.

If one is conscious enough to create their own story, they will realize their story shares common traits with the stories of others. While we are all extraordinarily diverse individuals, we are also all remarkably similar. Whether our story is to dedicate our life to solving a problem in our world, to teach others, to protect those who are more vulnerable, to build something new that changes how we live, or to serve in some other way, there is typically a desire to contribute somehow. The intended contribution usually touches the lives of others, and this is no coincidence. As humans, we are designed to live in connection with others, to be influenced by what they contribute, and to influence them as well. However, if we never create our own story, we will never fully understand this.

Life Without Knowing Our Story

While knowing our own story is necessary for having true purpose, it isn't necessary for us to survive. As long as we eat and sleep, our basic needs are met and we make it to the next day. If we have large amounts of money, we can easily spend a lifetime experiencing the pleasures it provides without having any sense of what our story is. Eating an endless line of gourmet meals and sunbathing on private beaches at luxury resorts may feel good, but it requires no self-awareness at all, let alone any realization that perhaps we're meant to be doing something more with the life we were given. If this is all we do, life still falls short of our true potential, yet we survive, and by some definitions even prosper. But to feel a sense of purpose, none of these things will be enough, even if we wish they could be. This is because humans were made with the potential to do much more, and arguably are *meant* to do much more. We have always been able to function at a much higher level than our history of survival or the design of our society would suggest. But for many, this is difficult to believe. Why? Because so many of us don't realize we don't really know our own story.

Many of my students didn't know their own story because nothing in their world told them they needed one. And to be fair, they were able to navigate successfully in the artificial world of our education system, which bears little resemblance to the real world. But not knowing their story meant someone else would inevitably tell them what to do with their lives, often without them consciously realizing it. For my students, the most common message they were told was that they were meant to acquire money and status in our society. As I've mentioned before, this happens because it's a result of how our society is designed, and being in a business school reinforces this message even more. While we have the freedom to choose, powerful external forces can influence our decisions, and may at times directly make our decision for us. To make sure our own individual needs and intentions are respected in the process, we must have at least some idea of what our story is.

If we don't know our own story, life becomes an experience defined by someone other than us. Not knowing our story means we cannot authentically communicate to others who we are, or why we are here. At best, we define ourselves by our jobs, our status, the organizations we associate with, and the money we make, because there really isn't much else to say about ourselves. Without our own story, these are the only things left that define who we are. In fact, this is often how we let someone else tell us who we are, because all of these external attributes are part of our society's design. A person who doesn't know their own story will attach themselves to these things strongly, and not waste any opportunity to remind others they have them. They do this partly out of necessity. If others don't value these things, they will feel they are worth less. Their existence is always an insecure one; if not for these things, why does it even matter that they are here?

If not knowing our own story means someone else tells us what to do, then it also means the visions we create may not really be ours either. Without developing enough consciousness, it's impossible to know whether we're driving our life or whether we are the passenger watching someone else drive. If we follow what someone else tells us to do, we may feel like we have a genuine sense of purpose for a period of time, because many external rewards and voices of encouragement along the way may tell us our life is on the right path. But after enough time passes, a clearer, more conscious look in the rearview mirror of what has happened will occur. When looking back, seeing a path of purpose will provide a sense of genuine satisfaction that the time and effort was well spent. But seeing a path where someone else has been driving all along will bring feelings of disappointment and confusion. How did we not know we weren't the ones driving?

A curious pattern I noticed among my students was how many of them would completely change their intended career path once they began interviewing for jobs. At first, I thought I was simply witnessing their progression in becoming more aligned with the story of their life. However, I soon realized I was mistaken. Sometimes they changed because some opportunities just didn't come, and they felt they had no choice but to move on to something else. But I also noticed the opposite occurred. A student may have started with little expectation or interest in a specific job, but if they got the job offer their interest increased dramatically if many of their peers were also competing for it. Because the job was coveted by so many of their classmates, they often felt blessed to be chosen out of the crowd. I knew the competitive structure of recruiting created the perception of a game of winners and losers, but I had underestimated its influence. I also failed to appreciate how persistent the idea of life as a constant state of competition would be. Long after graduation, I would discover many of my students believed they were still playing a game they needed to win, even if they were miserable contestants who would never get what they actually wanted. For better or worse, all of us are tempted by the desire to win competitions against our peers, which, in its unhealthy form, can serve as another powerful distraction to finding our own purpose.

10

THE AMAZING RAT RACE

*The trouble with the rat race is that
even if you win, you're still a rat.*
~ Lily Tomlin

How GOOD is your life? Maybe the day you got an A in the course you struggled with, a big bonus at work, or the new house you always wanted, life seemed pretty good. That is, until you found out the person next to you got an A+, over twice your bonus payout, and an unquestionably better house. While we might think answering the question of how good our life is should be based on our own judgment in isolation, most of us can't resist the temptation to compare ourselves to others in the outside world. When we compare ourselves to others, there's often a competitive aspect to the assessment. To be doing well, we need to have performed better on the measures we focus on relative to others. In its healthy form, competition with others gives us an idea of what's possible to achieve and motivates us to do better. But in its unhealthy form, it can become a trap with no genuine possibility of a happy ending, wasting enormous amounts of time and energy in a finite life.

The Value of Competitions

Competitions are an incredibly effective way of organizing humans in part because they have a remarkable simplicity to them. There are clear definitions of winners and losers, which easily allow individuals to be labeled as great, good, or not good enough. The rewards for winning are universally understood. All participants are given a common set of rules to follow, which allows their behavior to be dictated by an intentional design. The measures of performance used to determine winners also simplify what is otherwise a difficult problem to solve. How can we really tell one person is truly better than another at something that is too complicated to precisely define or measure? If taken seriously, the question is often challenging to answer, and can be almost philosophical in nature.

As a practical shortcut, competitions answer this question by using narrow and simple definitions. A better athlete is defined only by a few criteria or a single measure captured in a set period of time, although they may have other relevant but overlooked strengths. Promotions in a workplace may be granted to those who have higher evaluation scores, but the score may not reflect everything that would be considered important to label someone as truly better than another. Sometimes these shortcuts work well enough to provide a truthful answer to who is better, but in many cases, they are deliberate oversimplifications we use to make the process of deciding winners easier. Often, one is not truly worse than another even if they measure as less than someone else in a competition, but we need to believe this is true as a practical matter in order for a competition to have credibility. And more importantly, because competitions only work if winners and losers are narrowly defined, they always fail to recognize or appreciate the complexity of the individual participating, placing them in a box that is much smaller than who they really are.

Whether we are fully conscious of it or not, we are constantly put in circumstances that are competitions. Even from a young age our education system teaches us about competition, where grades are compared and the best-performing students are openly favored and rewarded. In work settings, the organizations we work for are actually a tournament, where over time fewer and fewer winners are promoted to move up in the hierarchy. Even outside of school and work, we often compete—for influence over others, praise from those we seek validation from, even the limited time of busy people we want to associate with. These competitions are not a product of nature, but are created entirely by us. Our competitions at school and work are an important feature of our society's design, but are not necessarily created for the primary purpose of benefitting individuals. Instead, these competitions are often an essential tool to organize individuals to achieve goals society and its institutions want to accomplish. This can be good for both society and the individual, as long as the individual understands what they want to obtain by participating and trying to win. However, the trouble begins when individuals aren't fully aware that a competition is actually an agreement between themselves and another entity that does not have their benefit as its main goal, and begin to confuse their own identity with the competition itself.

The Danger of Believing Competitions Define Our Identity

Without greater awareness, we can easily define ourselves by the scores we receive in every competition we've ever been in. If we got good grades in school, we can conclude we are surely very smart, and the opposite must also be true if we didn't. Believing this requires we ignore the fact that grades as a performance measure are far from perfect, and many more types of intelligence exist than what is usually measured in school. There is a seductive convenience in simply believing the measure tells us how smart we are. If someone else is promoted over us, it can be difficult to dismiss the idea they are better than us, especially if the decision was based on the collective vote of many people we know. Even if the promotion may also reflect factors other than one's competence in their work, it's much more convenient for everyone to operate on the belief the better candidate was chosen. When we are placed in boxes with clear labels on the outside that say how good we are, we feel a powerful temptation to believe they accurately identify us, even if they're not accurate at all. This is especially true if we don't have any other definition of ourselves outside of the competitions we participate in.

The students who came to my office encompassed the entire range of how much one could define themselves by the competitions they participated in. Many knew they were playing someone else's game, but were unsure of what to do about it. Others defined themselves completely by the competitions they participated in, and their happiness and self-worth were determined entirely by their performance at any given moment. However, regardless of how they defined themselves, if my students with full-time jobs had the expectation of upcoming promotion opportunities or more money, this served as a powerful magnet pulling them to stay on their current path. These upcoming rewards signaled they were winning the tournament, and were valued. A closer look at the ladders they were climbing revealed that staying a short while longer for additional rewards was rarely a short-term decision, even if it appeared to be. Staying usually reflected a decision to sign up to play the whole game. If the next promotion or payout didn't come, the tournament had succeeded in getting the most out of them that it wanted, and the next level of rewards would motivate those who were still moving up. If the rewards kept coming, staying a few years could turn into staying for much longer. There is nothing wrong with this system from the perspective of employers, because hierarchies are designed to influence our decisions about the future to serve their own goals. The tournament is also much less concerning if we enjoy and feel a sense of purpose in our work, and may even challenge us to grow in what we are meant to do. But if we are miserable at work, as many of the students in my office were, these competitions can create painful conflicts inside us.

Even if we define our entire identity by the competitions we participate in, we have the capacity to become conscious of the fact that our individuality is somehow being compromised. The initial warning almost never comes from the rational mind, but from our emotions. An uncomfortable sense of dissatisfaction can quickly grow into unhappiness, although it's often not obvious in the beginning why these feelings are emerging. While this can happen at any time along one's path, it's more likely to occur after a string of significant successes or significant failures. Ironically, experiencing success instead of failure doesn't prevent these emotions from growing, because the source of these feelings has nothing to do with external validation and rewards. They are a message from somewhere inside us that something important has been ignored for too long by the decisions we've made, even if our conscious mind has no idea what it is.

In the moment our emotions start to tell us something is wrong, the outside world often pressures us to dismiss them. If we've even partially defined our identity by the competitions we participate in, we may feel compelled to continue participating even if these competitions don't provide what we really need. We may think they are an important part of us, and who would we be if we left them? Without the job title, would we want to see what's left? Maybe the job has justified and hidden issues in our lives that we would rather avoid facing. We may also pursue fleeting experiences of pleasure to compensate for the negative emotions we feel, which is analogous to taking aspirin for chronic headaches. The pain can be reduced for periods of time, but will never really go away without addressing the root cause. We may consult with those we trust, but if we speak to others who have defined their identity by measures of the external world, we may be told we think too much, that we should just be grateful for what we have, or receive other unhelpful advice. All of this works to deny the signals coming from our emotions, setting the stage for a battle inside of us, with nothing less than the meaning of our life at stake.

The Voices in Our Head

To the outside world, we all appear to have only a single voice in our mind because we only possess one voice to speak out loud.

Inside of us, however, something much more complicated and messy takes place. Often, multiple voices are speaking in our head, each representing a distinct perspective. People who meditate for the first time or otherwise experience an increase in consciousness will often become aware of these different voices, which may sound like they have a mind of their own. If one gives it enough thought, this raises two related questions. If *we* are able to listen to the chatter of these voices in our head which seem to have a mind of their own, *Who are they and where do they come from?* This is a question of incredible practical importance, because when the voices disagree with each other and begin to battle inside us, a decision must be made about who to follow.

Many voices in our head are implanted from a young age. They might include the voices of our parents or other members of our family, our peers, or others who made a strong impression on us as we were growing up. As we become adults, new voices may emerge from other people we meet who make a profound impact on us in a moment of openness and vulnerability, both for better and worse. These voices embody a consistent perspective associated with the original individual, and can remain with us for our entire lives. The voices speak endlessly, commenting about situations both real and imagined, and may also regularly make judgments about our worth. This is less problematic if the voices in our head are loving, supportive, and empower us. Such voices can energize us when we face difficult challenges in our lives. But if they are critical, consistently negative, and judge us to be of little value, they can cripple us while we're trying to move forward on our own path. When someone defines their entire identity by the competitions they participate in, this often occurs not only due to a lack of consciousness, but also because the negative voices in their head dominate the narrative of who they are. These voices refuse to be satisfied directly by the individual, which creates the need to seek out validation from the external world. And our society offers no shortage of competitions where the validation of their value can be provided, as long as one is willing to pay the price for it.

Many of the students who came to my office weren't sure how to resolve the conflict between the different voices in their head. While the conflicts differed based upon the situation, by far the most common disagreement was between the voice of their emotions and a second voice that wanted to ignore their emotions. The first voice would regularly tell them they were on the wrong path; the second voice would provide a list of reasons why they could not and should not deviate from their current path. I noticed the second voice was often a more complex entity, appearing at first to sound completely reasonable with logical arguments, but which became increasingly unreasonable if it felt like it was losing the battle as the conversation progressed. At first, I didn't understand why this was happening, although the change in behavior struck me as odd. But after a long-enough discussion, I could hear a clearly identifiable voice. The voice I heard was a critical, negative voice implanted in my students' minds, which they had hidden away from the outside world, and which demanded external validation from competitions in order to be satisfied. However, my students were usually not aware of how dominant this voice was in dictating their lives, and how it compelled them to continue to win competitions that could never give them what their emotions were telling them was missing.

Life is ultimately not a competition, and was never intended to be. The way our society is structured, however, makes it easy to think our identity and value are based on our performance in competitions, even if they are someone else's imperfect creations. This is especially easy to believe if we are winning. If we're not conscious enough, we also cannot distinguish the sound of our own voices from the other implanted voices that live in our minds. But if our entire identities are based upon our performances in the competitions we participate in, our own voices are probably not the ones deciding our lives, and we may spend enormous amounts of time and energy pursuing things that fail to provide a genuine sense of purpose. If our emotions give us clear and consistent signals something is wrong, it's because something truly is wrong. As individuals, we are all supposed to walk a unique path, one that can never be entirely defined by the competitions created by others. Without being fully aware of all this, however, an understandable temptation exists to keep running in the rat race for the next level of rewards, although it will ultimately do nothing to silence the voice of our emotions.

The students with full-time jobs who came to my office were nowhere near the end of their lives, but I could see the trajectories they had chosen and the increasing challenges they had in switching their paths as they got older. They often made significantly more money each year that went by, and many simultaneously grew progressively less happy with their lives. I also began to notice something that struck me as odd. Some of my older students who had already made substantial sums of money were miserable, and were well past the point of being motivated by dopamine and fear. And yet, they continued walking on the same path despite the strong and consistent signals their emotions gave them. Andrew was a student of mine who was a particularly extreme example, who by his early thirties had already accumulated enough wealth to retire comfortably yet continued to live a tortured life in his job. I don't use the word torture lightly—he would ultimately come to my office multiple times, with each subsequent visit bringing an increased sense of desperation and hopelessness that started with how he saw his job, and expanded into how he saw his whole life.

These students were particularly puzzling to me at first, until I began to realize perhaps one of the most significant costs of the system we have created: many of my students kept persisting in their paths despite being unhappy simply because they knew no other way. They only knew what they knew.

11

YOU ONLY KNOW
WHAT YOU KNOW
(AND YOU DON'T KNOW
WHAT YOU DON'T KNOW)

The only true wisdom is in knowing you know nothing.
~ Socrates

It may seem obvious to say that as humans we only know what we know, but in practice we usually fail to consider this fact seriously. Instead, we often think we know more than we really do, which has practical value in helping us make decisions in our daily lives.[33] If we believed we knew nothing about a subject but needed to make a decision about it, we would have to spend the time and energy to educate ourselves or knowingly decide blindly. If we have to make many decisions like this, we risk becoming paralyzed or too entangled in constant analysis to productively move forward. It's often much easier to operate on the belief we know more than we do rather than consider our knowledge may be limited. Even if we aren't overconfident about how much we know, we usually still fail to comprehend what the limitations of our knowledge really mean about what we can do in the world, beyond the tiny corner of it we see immediately in front of us.

We Know What We See, Which Shapes What We Choose

The fact that we only know what we know has important implications, all of which determine our lives in ways we usually don't realize. One is that what an individual sees in their world will strongly predict the path they choose in life. The good, bad, ugly, and extraordinary in their world will all be relevant; they create one's understanding of reality, and what one chooses to do with their life will always be influenced by this reality. As I've mentioned before, observing the choices of others around them will offer especially convincing evidence of the choices they believe they have. It's understandably difficult to see things in any other way, because the information in our immediate environment is what we feel we can trust the most. What else could be more true, other than what we see with our own eyes? Understanding the nature of reality beyond what's right in front of us requires a level of thinking that is almost never actively encouraged or, for some, even allowed. Predictably, if a small world is placed in front of us, we may live a more limited life in almost every way. However, if a larger world is placed in front of us, the possibilities we perceive and the choices we believe we have expand.

Knowledge to Evolution

While the world we see immediately in front of us can completely determine the path of our life, it doesn't have to work this way. Humans can make the choice to learn things they don't know, which allows them to form new ideas and change old ones. This ability is one reason why growing up in negative and limiting environments doesn't always predict what happens in someone's life. We can increase what we know, and begin to see more than what's right in front of us. This knowledge increases our power as human beings if we are limited by our immediate environment, and makes it more likely we will grow to shape our environment rather than let our environment shape us. The reason our power increases is because of how knowledge affects the creation of our visions. No matter how original visions may appear to be, they are always based on the foundation of knowledge we have. Growing our foundation allows us to see more roads and more doors to what's possible in life, and create visions that look radically different from our current environment. This is nothing less than a form of human evolution, where who we were yesterday doesn't have to be who we are tomorrow, if we can expand what we know today.

However, expanding our knowledge isn't just about becoming conscious of the existence of other possibilities for us. We must also know how we feel about these possibilities emotionally. Why? Because emotions serve as the fuel for everything we do as humans. If we do something that makes us feel good, the emotion powers us forward. If we do something that creates only negative emotions, we are forever burdened as we try to advance, much like trying to climb a mountain with a heavy weight chained to our ankle. If we desire to follow a path that gives a genuine feeling of success and a strong sense of purpose, we must listen to the signals that come from our emotions and understand their messages. However, this creates a challenge, because at the outset, we may not have a clear idea of how we truly feel about doing something unless we actually do it. The price of gaining this knowledge can vary drastically depending on what's at stake. If we want to know how we feel about playing a new sport we've never tried before, it costs relatively little time and energy for us to try it out for an afternoon and see how we feel. The commitment in this case is small. But when we choose careers, the cost of trying to see how we feel about different paths often takes years of our life.

Testing for Emotional Signals

The earliest significant opportunity to try out different career paths often begins with our first job after finishing school, when the cost of switching careers and life paths is relatively low.[34] Having guides can significantly shorten the time and energy we spend testing out different career paths to understand how we feel. Of course, no true substitute exists for direct experience; it's the only real way to know what emotions will emerge from inside us. And ultimately, that's the whole point—we need to know what our emotions say about each path we're trying. With most types of work, there will be a mix of experiences that bring both positive and negative emotions. Consciously weighing the balance of these emotions and factoring them into how we make our pivotal life decisions is absolutely critical. All of this may sound obvious, but in practice very few of my students followed this approach. Instead, they often leaned heavily on their rational mind to make their decisions, weighing factors including money and prestige, as well as the opinions of those around them. When it came to their emotions, they would often try to change them to be as positive as possible to support their decision, in some cases ignoring clear warnings their emotions were trying to communicate. Tuning out the outside world and tuning in to their own emotions was an exercise I rarely saw my students do. Unless, ironically, I persuaded them to do so.

The years immediately after completing school are both exciting and scary, in part because they are the first taste of both real freedom and real responsibility. This time period fundamentally shapes the path every individual ultimately takes in life, although how this occurs is only obvious much later. This is also the time when most of us will create many of the defining principles and beliefs we will carry for a lifetime. With enough consciousness, these years provide the cheapest and easiest opportunity for us to start building a bridge to the life we want to have. We may discover our first job, or even first several jobs after graduation are not for us, and we may learn something important about ourselves we didn't know before. This is simply the process at work as we find our way. As we go through the process we need to know what emotions we feel and why, which we can only really know from direct experience. However, the opportunity to explore during these years can also be squandered if we are unconscious or too distracted. What's the difference between the individual who begins building a bridge in the right direction and one who squanders the opportunity? For my students, the difference was the knowledge they possessed. All of my students only knew what they knew and operated from their knowledge, but what they knew about possibilities in life and the importance of listening to their emotions differed considerably.

As an example, Rebecca and Daniel were two students of mine with full-time jobs who had grown progressively less happy at work. Rebecca's father was a serial entrepreneur who loved building businesses, so much so that he spent less than a year in retirement before starting yet another new venture. Knowing firsthand that it was possible for one to enjoy their work, Rebecca was already exploring new career options by the time she visited my office, and would ultimately change careers soon after graduation. By contrast, both of Daniel's parents were lawyers who didn't enjoy their work; most of his childhood memories included seeing adults just like his parents, well-paid professionals who all worked long hours and seemed unhappy. This is what Daniel understood to be normal, and as a consequence didn't interpret his negative emotions as a warning sign.

Knowledge Shapes Our Path

The knowledge we possess is a powerful predictor of how we evolve and ultimately express our identity in the world. How much knowledge we have comes partly from the environments we experience, but also from whether we choose to expand our knowledge beyond what's right in front of us. If an individual is continuously growing their foundation of knowledge, their identity and understanding can change radically as their life progresses. Small dreams can become big dreams, old beliefs can be traded for new ones, and a life with no direction can find purpose. By contrast, having a foundation of knowledge that does not grow will mean a person remains exactly the same as they grow older. This difference in evolution becomes easier to observe as individuals age, when the gap becomes too obvious to ignore. In each case however, they only know what they know. And, they typically also don't know what they don't know. Humans are not all equally aware of the possibilities in life or what they are capable of. I see it all the time as a teacher. I often see the potential students have, but also how their choices fall short of their potential. I've often wondered what would happen if only they could see just a little bit more than the world right in front of them.

For many of the students who came to my office who chose to remain in their full-time jobs despite being miserable, their understanding of reality had grown narrower over the years, and their immediate environment was all they could see in the world. Their emotions had grown louder and louder, telling them their current path was wrong, but their foundation of knowledge had failed to grow enough to reveal any new paths. Because of the way our society is designed, their attempts to address these personal challenges were usually a lonely journey, leaving them vulnerable to distractions and unhelpful guidance from those who did not understand them or have a genuine interest in their well-being. But I also noticed a pattern, especially among the older students who came to my office. In many cases, by the time they had come to see me their quality of life had been steadily declining for a long period of time, well beyond what could have been considered a temporary situation. Part of this was due to knowing only what they knew, but I also noticed there was another reason. Over the years, they had consistently chosen to follow the path of least resistance in life, riding on the inertia from decisions made long ago. Without realizing it, they had dug themselves into a hole which only grew deeper over time, by their own hands.

12

GOING THROUGH LIFE
ON AUTOPILOT

Consciousness is only possible through change;
change is only possible through movement.
~ Aldous Huxley

Is human life a state of constant change and learning, or are we creatures of habit simply repeating the same familiar routines?

Once we become used to doing something regularly in our lives, it often becomes part of our ability to fly on autopilot, where we no longer need to be fully conscious in order to accomplish what's in front of us. All of us have the ability to switch on our autopilot, and once we do, a natural temptation to sit back and fall asleep overtakes us. Our full attention is, it would seem, no longer necessary. But while asleep, we miss everything we otherwise would have seen if we were awake during the journey. We don't see the signs and people pointing to important opportunities meant for us. We fail to notice even the most obvious warnings about where we're headed if they appear. Even an appreciation for the journey itself, understanding it as an important part of the experience of living, is lost because our eyes are closed. While on autopilot, there is very little chance for new thinking or insight because we cannot see anything new to consider. Not surprisingly, when we're in this state, nothing in our life really changes.

While good arguments can be made for both perspectives—that life is a state of constant change and learning and that we are also creatures of habit—the reality is, we are not only one or the other, but always a mixture of both. This mixture creates a tension inside us, where we may want to make changes to improve our life but still feel comfortable doing the same things we've become accustomed to. The novelty of change can be exciting, scary, or both. If change leads to a desired outcome, we will experience positive emotions which reinforce the idea that we can transform our lives for the better. At the same time, staying within our routines provides a sense of comfort that comes with familiarity. The life we choose to live depends upon how we manage the tension between these desires, because they will forever represent contradictory demands.

For most of us, only very rarely do we make significant changes to our vision, and on most days, we can be seen following our familiar routines. This can have immense practical benefit. If we want to accomplish any meaningful goals, we will almost always need regular work routines to get us there, which we have to maintain consistently over time. But we may also follow the same routines we had yesterday without meaningful goals. This happens because our routines were created to support decisions made in the past under different circumstances. They may have been reasonable given what was known at the time, but circumstances eventually change, and our foundation of knowledge may also have expanded. After enough time, routines that were once sensible may no longer make sense. This can lead to an odd situation, if one believes humans possess great power through the gift of free will: We may appear to be busy in our lives every day, but are no longer evolving or working to accomplish visions. This is a life lived on autopilot.

Losing Consciousness

One reason we may still continue to follow the same routines but no longer work toward meaningful goals is that we've become less conscious over time, paying attention only to what's immediately in front of us every day. This is an unintended negative consequence of what is usually a benefit from having routines. As we continue to repeat our routines, the amount of conscious effort required decreases, and we may reach the point of being able to execute them without being fully aware of what we're doing. If we experience little joy in our working lives, our decreased awareness can also provide a way to cope with doing what we would rather not do, because we will no longer experience it as consciously. After a long-enough period of time this type of withdrawal can lead to a state of numbness, where the emotional highs and lows experienced at work become diminished because one is no longer fully present. Whether we reach this state and the length of time we remain in it ultimately depends upon how we approach our life.

The Passive Approach to Living

If one approaches their life passively, then by definition the universe determines their life. If the forces of the universe push them left, they go left. If they are instead pushed another way, then that way is the path of their life. To some degree this cannot be controlled, and at certain times it will feel as if all of it is out of our control, and we are merely a puppet directed by a larger power above us, pulling the strings that command us without our consent. The influence of the universe in our lives does not mean human life is inevitably a passive existence, but taking a passive approach to life will convince us this is true because it's entirely self-fulfilling. It will lead us to react to what the universe appears to give or take away, but give no inspiration to proactively try and change what we see in our world. Every experience will reinforce the idea that life is determined by the universe and not by us, because there will be no evidence that significant intentional change is possible. If we simply follow what we believe is already laid out in front of us by the universe, then whatever happens next is not really our doing, but the will of the universe.

Taking a passive approach to life is not only self-fulfilling, it also has a profound effect on the benefit we receive from gaining additional knowledge. While expanding our knowledge is the most effective way to increase our power because of how it affects our ability to create visions, a passive approach to living can take this power away. If we possess knowledge but do not apply it deliberately in our lives, there is no benefit at all to knowing. We may read a thousand books on a subject to improve our lives, but if we maintain a passive approach to how we live, what we know intellectually will change nothing. It's the lifestyle equivalent of being in a coma. This is easy to observe in our world because there is no shortage of individuals who acquire life-changing knowledge only to live exactly the same way they did before. Because of this, it isn't enough to increase our foundation of knowledge to feel genuine success and a strong sense of purpose. We must take action—put one foot in front of the other and get moving—for our own sake.

If we take a passive approach to life, acknowledging we are doing so is understandably uncomfortable. If we are unsatisfied with our lives, it's far easier to point to external forces in the universe as the reason for our circumstances instead of pointing to ourselves as having somehow chosen our circumstances. Of course, the truth is our life is a joint outcome of us and the forces of the universe, with neither side in full control of the story. But it can be tempting to say we are not responsible for the story, and point to crucial moments where the universe pushed against our intentions and free will as clear evidence. Identifying ourselves as victims is easier than admitting we are at least partly responsible for why we did not get to where we desired, especially when it seems morally justified. It may also seem easier than considering what our next intentional steps should be, especially if we have not engaged in any true self-reflection. The danger of adopting this belief is that it takes the experiences of specific moments and incorrectly assumes the remainder of our lives will surely work the same way. This is false, although completely understandable. But our futures may indeed turn out as badly as we fear, only because life offers little reward for taking a passive approach.

Perhaps the most damaging aspect of choosing a passive approach to life is that it dramatically increases the chances of an unhappy existence. This is because of the way life itself is structured. If there were an equal chance of a good outcome occurring with both a passive and proactive approach to living, then it would be much less important how we approached it. However, the rewards life can offer are heavily biased to favor those who take a proactive approach. Little reward is offered to those who choose to be passive. This is not to say being proactive is easy or has no costs. In fact, it may be quite the opposite—a proactive approach to life often includes painful experiences and difficult challenges. But it's the only way to receive many of the good outcomes life can give. Life is structured to reward intentional effort, which is necessary to accomplish the visions we create for ourselves. A passive approach ignores this fundamental structure, which then alters the course of our lives. It is choosing to resign as co-creators of our own lives and telling the universe to do the work.

Trouble then begins to grow. The universe we perceive that pulls our strings from above becomes an indifferent or oppressive power. We then find ourselves walking along a dark path, much like descending deep into a dungeon with no bottom level. Trudging forward with no light, no guidance, and no clear intention, the mind will raise a question: What is the point of all this? There will be no satisfying answer to this question, because taking a passive approach denies the basic structure of how life works, where only intentional effort leads to better outcomes. We need to find our way out of the dungeon. Fundamentally, we are meant to take a proactive approach to life, simply because doing so aligns with life's design.

My students each had their own unique balance between their desires for both change and familiarity. However, some of my older students with full-time jobs had grown less happy over time in part because they had stayed too long in their comfortable routines. They felt unfulfilled at work, but their preference for familiarity had led to multiple missed opportunities to change the course of their lives.

As one example, David was a student of mine who had grown

tired of the repetitive work he did as a programmer for a major technology company, but also repeatedly ignored opportunities to try something new that his many friends from college offered. Initially puzzled by his behavior, I learned he had passed on these opportunities not out of fear, but because going to work doing the same thing he did yesterday was somehow easier on any given day than making a substantive change. The force of inertia had lulled him into an idle slumber. Days had turned into months, and months had turned into years. He had chosen to take a passive approach to life, to descend blindly into the dungeon.

But the story didn't always end there. For some of my students, I witnessed significant changes they would make in the direction of their lives, all of which took them closer to what was their own true path. I learned that change is always possible. No matter how lost they were, they could set an intention and begin to find a way out. In every case, it was a moment of clarity—an awakening—that raised their level of consciousness and defined their turning point.

PART II

Evolution

13

A MOMENT OF AWAKENING

We don't see things as they are; we see them as we are.
~ Anonymous

One of the most rewarding aspects of being a teacher is witnessing the moment your students truly understand what you've taught them. That's when their faces of frustration and indifference fade, and their eyes widen just a little because a light bulb has just turned on in their mind. Learning is a process where one's patience is tested at least as much as their intellect, with long periods of struggle where one has only a vague and imprecise understanding of a subject. These periods of struggle are sprinkled with occasional moments of clarity, where suddenly everything comes together and makes sense. Once a student reaches that moment, they are forever changed. In the classroom, these moments reflect greater understanding of subject matter knowledge. But for the students who visited my office, I witnessed a very different kind of clarity, where their hesitation would turn into excitement once they saw the direction they should take. I realized these one-on-one moments in my office were much more important than the moments in my classroom, because they could lead my students to entirely different lives.

Awakening from the Outside

If the only reason we repeat the same routines without a clear vision is a lack of consciousness, then immediate and dramatic change is possible. To begin the process of change, only an increase in the level of consciousness is required, much like waking from a nap. Once awake, we can naturally adjust our direction and effort, and once again move forward in our lives with conscious intention. One way for this to occur is if an external force in our environment stimulates us, where we receive a clear sign we have fallen asleep and realize we are going in the wrong direction. Before I became a professor, the most common version of this I observed was when individuals lost members of their family, partners, or other loved ones. These tragic and profound events sometimes led to significant changes in their lives soon after. Some were coworkers who quit and left our office, withdrawing from the repetitions of our daily grind to find another world. Others were friends or classmates from school, who would dramatically change their paths and lives in ways that surprised everyone around them. In each case, the loss of someone close to them had brought them closer to the reality of death, touching something inside them which began to reveal itself. Once it did, change became necessary because they could see their current direction was clearly wrong.

An external stimulus doesn't only originate from losing someone close to us; it can come from anything, anyone, and anywhere. It can be much gentler, but lead to similarly dramatic changes because one is already ready to change course. In these cases, the external stimulus strengthens a feeling already growing inside us. I noticed this was exactly what some of the students who visited my office were looking for, whether they realized it or not. The pressure they felt inside them had already reached a boiling point; they were eager to change direction. But they were waiting, in a kind of holding pattern. Sometimes they needed confirmation, or encouragement to hear they were not crazy. Other times, it wasn't a sanity check they needed, but permission to change their current path. I was stunned the first few times I experienced this, and began to see how deeply our system had embedded its own commands and values in my students. They had the genuine freedom to choose, but at the same time were afraid to deviate from what they believed was expected of them. This fear was not a character flaw or failure on their part, but a product of the conditioning they received. It is the conditioning we have all received.

An increase in consciousness doesn't only come from a stimulus from the external world; it can also happen in other ways. Some of the students who visited my office experienced it during our meetings, which was extraordinary to witness. It was like watching them complete a puzzle, putting in the final pieces to see a map that would tell them where they were meant to go. They were no longer lost. But how did this happen? Even if I saw the final pieces come together in my office, I knew they had already done most of the work before they visited me. All we had done was put the finishing touches on what was already well underway. The reason this happened wasn't because they were any smarter or more capable than any of my other students. Instead, they had found ways, either by luck or through deliberate effort, to understand themselves better.

Good and Bad Guides

Some of us are fortunate enough to have genuinely good guides in life. They help us see ourselves more clearly and make sense of the uncertain road ahead. They help us get to where we want to go, and to do so successfully. Guides come in all forms and degrees of quality. Some guides teach us the values and principles that will help us create our visions. Others tell us what we can expect from fellow humans in the world, which will influence who we choose to trust and how we conduct ourselves around different people. Other types of guides are experts we rely upon for a specific set of situations or challenges, who usually have been through a version of what we're dealing with. Some may genuinely care about us as individuals, and some may offer their help because we are useful to them somehow. Because they only know what they know, each guide will provide insight based only on their own experiences and knowledge, and nothing more. But in order to be a good guide, it's not enough to genuinely care about an individual or be supremely knowledgeable. What all good guides have in common is sufficient understanding of the individual they are trying to help. They know everyone is unique, and they understand what's unique about the person they're giving guidance to.

Although it took some time to notice the pattern, I realized many of my students had chosen to follow guides who had failed them by pointing them in the wrong direction, at least when it came to their happiness at work. This was almost never due to intentional misdirection of any kind, since virtually all the guides my students had chosen only wanted what was best for them. The failure was based on a mistaken assumption; the guides thought they knew what my students really needed and wanted out of life, and my students made the same assumption by asking for their guidance in the first place. As one might expect, these guides projected their own values and beliefs onto them because that's all they knew. What else could be expected? But after getting to know many of my students, I learned that when it came to one's pivotal life decisions, the chances of having good guides in life were perhaps not that high. If we are all so unique, then it takes real time and effort to get to know someone, and to do so without imposing our own values and beliefs is even harder. For my students who had found such guides, it was neither brilliance nor hard work that made them appear, but simply blessed luck.

Ironically, I observed that both good and bad guides could lead to increased consciousness. Good guides helped my students to adopt the right foundation and principles, or gently revealed that what they imagined about different possible life paths was far from reality. They had helped my students move forward in the right direction, and avoid some of the painful experiences that would have come with a trial-and-error approach. Moving forward on the right path led to experiences that increased their self-awareness along with their confidence, as they came to understand who they were. Bad guides had done the exact opposite, and my students had followed what they thought was good advice only to experience emptiness, pain, or both. These emotions also led to an increase in self-awareness, similar to how feeling a sharp pain in one's leg suddenly causes one to focus on it and investigate to find a cure. Many of these students ended up in my office, and I began to see their challenge was they didn't really understand the true nature of what caused their pain.

Good and bad guides bring different risks which can prevent one from finding their own true path. While having good guides is certainly a blessing, it can create an over-dependence on the guide and the loss of one's true sense of self. No guide is meant to lead you all the way to your true path—at best, they can only provide important clues and puzzle pieces. But when faced with an uncertain future, it's human nature to follow someone's guidance if it has served you well in the past, and a temptation exists to stop looking within for answers. The most frightening moment for individuals in this position is when the guide is no longer around to lead them, and they lose confidence in how to proceed. This is not how life was designed to work. Good guides teach us to grow into who we are supposed to be, to live a life of purpose, but not to serve as a substitute for the conscious steps we must take on our journey.

While having bad guides can lead to increased consciousness, the danger is, one may fail to understand what's really happening to them once they become more aware. If they feel pain, they naturally will begin to investigate the cause with the intention of finding a cure, but may not clearly see the true cause. Pain provides a signal with limited information, but is almost never a leap into full understanding. For example, we might experience physical pain in our stomach, but on its own the pain doesn't clearly tell us what the cause is. We need to be aware of any other unusual symptoms we might have, consider the most likely explanations, and perhaps even consult a doctor to help us understand what's happening inside us. But if one is surrounded by others who also have no understanding of the true cause, let alone the cure, they may struggle to gain any insight. If one cannot clearly see, asking others who also cannot see does little to help. For most of my students, this was the world they lived in. Those around them had limited consciousness, and the signals from their emotions were poorly understood and almost never openly discussed. My students needed to understand what was happening and why it was happening. What brought many of them to my office was their desperation to find someone—anyone—who could help.

Awakening from Within

Aside from following guides, some of my students raised their own consciousness by building a solid foundation of knowledge which they continuously worked to expand. Their foundation came from many different sources, which they were unafraid to explore even if the implanted voices in their head tried to discourage them. They also often engaged in regular practices and rituals that increased their consciousness, including meditation, yoga, or writing in a daily journal. For these students, a powerful external stimulus wasn't needed for them to understand who they were and where they were headed. In spite of the many distractions our society threw at them to get their attention, they had set aside time and space for themselves to regularly turn off the external noise in their world. Just like how one can tell someone with a well-developed physique has a high level of discipline in maintaining their physical fitness, I could tell my students who followed these practices operated at a different level of awareness than their peers. They asked different questions, and could see further beyond what was immediately in front of them. They were less reactive to the events and competitions in their life, and more proactive about making sure the road they were on was really their path and not one imposed on them. And, although it took time to witness it, they ended up with a sense of confidence in expressing themselves in the paths they chose. They had evolved to a life of purpose, or at the very least come closer to it.

In my early years as a professor, I naively thought simply having a moment of awakening was all that was needed to change course for a better direction, and that this alone would diminish whatever fears and worries my students had. Surely, seeing themselves and the road ahead a little more clearly was enough? Except that it wasn't, as I saw what happened to many of my students in the years that followed. While they were all understandably afraid to some degree of changing their path, for some the fear had crippled them, and for others, they somehow managed to move forward despite their fear and change the course of their lives. Only after observing this pattern repeat itself over and over again did I begin to see something that fundamentally separated those who really lived their own lives, and those who never could. It wasn't their fears; it was their courage.

14

THE POWER OF COURAGE

I have learned over the years that when one's mind is made up,
this diminishes fear; knowing what must be done does
away with fear.
~ *Rosa Parks*

Fear is one of the greatest obstacles we face within ourselves in following our own path, and as I've mentioned before can paralyze us from moving forward. But it isn't *feeling* fear that is the obstacle, although it may seem like this surely must be the problem. Some people may hide their fear while others are more open, but everyone experiences fear when breaking away from the expectations placed on them to follow their own path. This is especially true if there is little encouragement from the external world. I never saw a student in my office who wasn't at least a little afraid when they decided to change course to do what they really wanted to do, even if they could clearly see it was the right answer for them. Feeling fear is only natural. But fear can be a paralyzing obstacle to expressing ourselves and manifesting our visions, not because we feel it, but because we do not fully understand its nature or how to manage it. We may also not know where to find the courage to follow our own path; this is actually part of a larger problem—many of us struggle to understand and manage not just our fears, but all of our emotions.

Perhaps the greatest failure of our education system is how little we are taught in school about our emotions and how to manage them.[35] If we don't understand our emotions, we often unconsciously believe our emotions are what define us. If we are happy, sad, angry, or afraid then that must be who we are. A lack of awareness dictates this. However, we are not our emotions. If one has ever entered an extreme state of any emotion, they may realize their thoughts and behavior change significantly in these emotional states, to the point where they may become unrecognizable to themselves. Emotions can serve as signals; they may feel good or bad, and they may motivate us to behave in certain ways, but they are not who we are. A separate *you* exists, and this you has been here all along.

The Two Extremes of Responding to Fear

If our emotions are not us, what are we supposed to do when we experience them? If the emotions are negative, the most convenient responses represent two extremes, both of which are understandable if one isn't at a higher level of consciousness. At one extreme, we can simply act out and express our emotions with little control. The benefit of this? We are connected to our emotions. However, we're also in a constant state of only reacting to events and interactions with others, which leads to these external factors dictating our entire life experience. Those who operate in this way will find they often experience events or do things in a way they come to regret later. They may say things like "I wish I didn't worry so much back then" or "I really wish I hadn't done that, but I wasn't feeling great." At the other extreme, we may avoid or suppress our emotions in order to function productively and accomplish our goals. This can work for a period of time, but leads to other negative consequences. If we always avoid whatever triggers negative emotions inside us, our world will begin to shrink as we withdraw, and we will grow increasingly isolated. If we suppress our emotions, they become increasingly difficult to manage, and will eventually interfere with our ability to function. It's the equivalent of pushing down tightly on the lid of a boiling pot, where we must press harder and harder to keep everything contained as the pressure inside increases. These responses are not very effective at managing our emotions, and will only produce a limited quality of life. But without learning any other way, they are the most natural choices we have.

When we experience feelings of fear, the two easiest ways to respond correspond with the same two extremes, where we may either become consumed by it or avoid what we are afraid of entirely. What I often observed in my students was either the fear of repeating painful failures in their past, or the fear of the worst-case scenario happening in their search for a job after graduation. Perhaps they would end up unemployed after receiving their expensive degree and unable to survive, or at the very least fail to get the job they had hoped for. The longer the uncertainty about the final outcome dragged on and the more setbacks they experienced in the interim, the more tortured they became. The tortured were a significant fraction of my students, especially in years where jobs were scarce due to the economy, although I never saw anyone ultimately finish unemployed. It was in these moments that I felt both the greatest sympathy and the most powerless to help my students, although as the years passed I learned these moments were not as defining as they and I had expected. But it was a seasonal part of my job to watch the levels of fear rise among them much like the high tide coming in, and to see it consume a fraction of each cohort coming through.

If my students were not consumed by fear, some did their best to avoid fearful situations, such as skipping job applications for certain employers to avoid the experience of being rejected. It's hard to be rejected when you reject them first. But I also saw this in my classroom. In every class I taught, there were bright students who rarely spoke in class if at all, even though a significant part of their final grade was based on participation. I knew they had a lot to say when I read what they submitted in their written assignments, and yet they remained quiet. Whenever I asked these students why they didn't participate, their answer was always the same. They didn't want to inadvertently say something that sounded stupid, especially in front of their classmates. They were afraid of being judged and found it safer to be quiet, even if there was no penalty to their grade for participating and a clear benefit to doing so. As I got to know more of my students with every year of teaching, I learned it wasn't just with job recruiting or class participation where they were avoiding something. Everyone has something they avoid out of fear, much like how one might hide a scar they feel embarrassed about.

Separating from Fear

What's a better way of dealing with fear, then? The first step is to clearly see its presence and behavior. This is necessary before focusing on courage, because courage does not extinguish fear at the outset. Fear demands your acknowledgement before it can be managed in an effective way. But greater consciousness of what's happening is needed. Without it, fear will automatically trigger a reaction inside you, like how tapping your knee triggers an immediate reflexive kick when you're being examined at the doctor's office. Tuning out the outside world and calming your mind, deepening and slowing your breath, and looking inside yourself to notice what's happening with the different emotions and voices in your head will give you the space to consciously interrupt and dampen the intensity of the reaction. The longer you stay in stillness and observe yourself—which is not easy for the uninitiated—the larger the space will grow. When doing this, don't get attached to any thoughts of a worst-case scenario playing out in your head; simply let them pass you by. You are increasing the awareness of your separation from the emotion you're feeling. Fear does not need to consume you. But it also cannot be ignored, even after you become aware of this.

One way to think about fear is that it likes to attach itself to our true identity when we're not paying attention to what's happening inside ourselves. However, once we become more conscious it naturally separates itself from us. But if it's still attached to us and we begin to react to it, the fear becomes energized and increases in intensity. The longer we react to it in this state the more intense the fear becomes, and our mind will create as many unpleasant and frightening things it can while it has our attention.

Naturally, we will also begin to react to these new thoughts. For my students who struggled to get the jobs they wanted, the many months of sending resumes, networking, interviews, and waiting to hear from employers gave ample opportunities for fear to grow in their minds, regardless of whether they were rational or not. These fears would sometimes be voiced out loud in my office. "What if I don't get to work for my top choice of employer?" and "What if I don't get a job in the industry I want?" and "Wait— what if I don't get a job *anywhere*?" Even if we increase our consciousness and our fear begins to separate from us, it will attempt to reattach itself to us at the next opportunity, patiently waiting until we lose consciousness again. If we do, it will become energized once more. We must work to maintain the separation, to keep an open space between us and the fear inside us. Instead of letting it consume us or avoiding whatever we fear, we observe it at a distance, from a new perspective. This sets the best conditions for courage to emerge.

Courage in the Face of Fear

Courage is the willingness to take action despite feeling fear, not the absence of fear. Like many things in life, finding the courage to do something we're afraid of doing appears to be a circular problem. We wouldn't need courage if we weren't afraid, and our fear would naturally diminish if we already had enough courage to move forward and persist, simply because we would gain confidence from experience. But at the outset, we don't have the luxury of having either situation. The problem is complicated further if we know there's a good chance our initial attempts at doing something we're afraid of will be painful. If someone has an irrational fear of leaving their home, an effective treatment can be to slowly increase their exposure to the outside world over time. With this approach, we can be confident they will gradually accept the fact that their fears wildly exaggerate the risk of bad outcomes. But our confidence in this approach is based on knowing being outside isn't so terrible, even the first time we attempt it. However, when making significant changes to our path in life the initial period after change is often legitimately challenging, and we often don't know how long that period will last. We cannot erase the fear we feel before deciding to change; the best we can do is manage it. So, courage is necessary to empower us to follow our own path. But where do we get it?

When deciding whether to pursue our own vision, courage ultimately comes from inside us. When our fear is substantial and we're facing a pivotal life decision, the roots of courage come from a combination of our story and philosophy of life. As I've mentioned before, the story of our life is the answer to the question of *why we exist*. It's closely related to the other fundamental question of life, "Who am I?" The story of our life may give us good reasons to be courageous, or offer little reason for why we should bother. If we're afraid of doing something but believe that doing it is why we exist, we have a foundation for courage, a reason to push forward. This provides the justification for why we must do it, even if our fear tells us to avoid it. We must know our story well and keep it in our conscious mind in order to have the ideal conditions for courage, because if we forget it our courage quickly fades. Once our story gives us a reason to do something, then the question that arises is how we should manifest it practically. This requires us to have a philosophy of life, which is our theory of how life works.

Our Philosophy of Life: We All Have a Theory

An important part of how science works is the testing of theories we have about the world. We don't know if our theories are true at the outset, but a lot of time and effort is spent trying to convincingly test them in the real world. Every individual also approaches life with their own personal theory, which describes how life itself works. Do we receive intentional signs from the universe telling us what we're supposed to do, or are the strange coincidences we experience simply randomness? Do we have a predetermined fate, or is it our choice what happens next? The decisions we make in life and the resulting consequences are tests of our theory. By the standards of good science though, they offer little evidence either proving or disproving whatever theory we have. Good scientific tests have a way of seeing what would happen if we *didn't* do what we decided, as well as providing lots of data points to help us build confidence that what we're seeing is accurate. But life doesn't offer these ideal conditions to test whether we're right about our own theories.[36] We will never really know for sure if our theories are correct, even by the end of our lives. Ironically, this is why it matters tremendously what theory we have. We all need a theory to operate in life, and our life experiences give us little chance to convincingly prove whether we are truly correct in our understanding. This leads to an odd, very unscientific conclusion: We may wish to choose a theory that improves our chances for a higher quality of life and not care at all about discovering how true it is, because we will never really know.

If the story of our life gives us a reason to pursue something despite our fear, then our philosophy of life will either confirm it or disagree. To create the ideal conditions for courage to emerge, the two must be in agreement. For example, if we believe that why we exist is to build something new that changes how we live, then we have a reason to be courageous and invest our time and energy into it, despite our fear of failure. However, if our theory is that the universe will make the road ahead difficult because an extraordinary amount of luck is needed to succeed in life, we may be less inclined to take the risk.[37] By contrast, if our theory is that the universe will help us because it responds positively to our intentions, we'll be more willing to take action. Which theory is true? I haven't a clue, and have seen plenty of evidence for both. But to show courage, the second theory is clearly the better choice.

As a practical matter, what is the most effective theory we can believe to be courageous? It's always some version of us needing to play the role of someone who actively manifests their visions, but having guidance and support from the external world. Some people move forward and take action believing there is a divine being, beings, or universal intelligence that directs them and helps them achieve what they want. Even if they don't manifest what they wanted, they continue to believe they are being guided and supported. Other people may take action with no belief in divine beings or forces, but still view the universe as a cooperative companion in helping them to manifest what they want in life. Of course, our philosophy of life is something that's deeply rooted inside us, and doesn't change easily because these are our core beliefs about how the world works. But if we could freely choose the theory that would give us the most courage, it's always some version of us needing to take action to achieve what we desire, with help from someone or something in the universe.

From Courage to Comfort

The beautiful thing about courage is, it doesn't need to last forever, because at some point with enough experience the fear of whatever we're doing fades away. We learn in a convincing way many of the terrible outcomes we were worried about don't happen, and we also become better at doing it over time. This is how everything we are afraid of works. What seems impossible or too painful later becomes part of the daily routine. What initially causes extreme anxiety later makes one comfortable, then eventually bored. It sounds bizarre because the actual activity hasn't changed at all, but we have. It's some of the clearest evidence that how we experience life is largely in our emotional responses to what we do, not really in the activities themselves. The better we become at managing our emotions, the better our lives can be.

My students developed their patterns of dealing with fear long before we had ever met. Some learned to avoid the things they feared, while others learned to face them repeatedly. Most students weren't at either extreme, but usually followed a unique mixture of both approaches. Their responses were shaped by their own individual experiences, which they took as lessons from their past. But blended in with their fear was a legitimate concern. Even if they faced their fears, it was still true that every pivotal decision they made in life had a certain amount of risk, even if it could not be precisely measured. Blindly ignoring risk probably wasn't the right answer to making good decisions in life, but neither was avoiding it at all costs. How were they supposed to think about it?

15

THE CURIOUS
CASE OF RISK

Life is either a daring adventure or nothing.
~ Helen Keller

While we cannot *know* beforehand what the outcome will be of the important decisions we make in life, we do know that every possible choice we make entails risk. Risk is part of the experience of living, and one of the main reasons why life can be so challenging. If there was no potential downside, no danger to anything we did, life would be much easier, although maybe it would also be uninteresting. We'd simply do whatever we wanted, no matter how outrageous it may seem, knowing we could never lose or face actual danger. Risk, or at least our perception of it, shapes how our decisions are framed; to consider the possibility of something less desirable occurring than our intended outcome. Even when creating our visions, the risks we perceive can influence what our vision ultimately looks like. However, despite the presence of risk in all of our life decisions, most of us are given little guidance on how to understand and manage it. We are left to figure it out for ourselves.

The Two Sides of Chris

Two students of mine had very different ways of approaching risk. One student, Chris, was cautious by nature—even his comments while participating in class were meticulous and precise, always reflecting the careful analysis he did before he spoke. He had concluded a career in tax accounting was the right choice because, according to him, "nothing is more certain than death and taxes." True to his plan, upon graduation he accepted a tax accounting job with a large global accounting firm. The whole process of getting a job had been, by his own admission, predictable and easy. But he hadn't come to my office to talk about being a tax accountant. It turned out he also had another interest.

Sitting in my office, he wore a blue pullover sweater and khaki pants, creating a conservative look that was a common sight within our school. He eyed my fake plants for a moment, which I had learned by now didn't calm anyone who visited my office. He took a deep breath after an awkward moment of silence and revealed something with the hushed tone of someone confessing to a terrible crime:

"I know I told you I want to be a tax accountant. But to be honest, I've always had another interest," he said. "I've always wanted to write fiction."

Inside my mind, I breathed a sigh of relief. Writing fiction wasn't an offense I was obligated to report to the school.

The rest of our conversation felt like I was speaking not to one, but two people in the room. "Accountant Chris" was the dominant personality, no-nonsense and confident. His views were validated by everything and everyone in the world around him: his grades in his accounting courses were excellent, he was a favorite student among his accounting professors, and his parents openly expressed their approval that he had chosen a well-paying and respectable profession that clearly justified his expensive degree. "Thank goodness you didn't become a starving artist," his father had joked.

But then there was "Author Chris." Much more timid, he was barely ever given a chance to speak. He had been constantly over-ruled because what he wanted was judged to be far too risky, and he didn't know how his writing would earn enough to make a living. Despite this, he had started writing a book, but gave up halfway through after feeling too discouraged. No one in Chris's environment had ever nurtured or encouraged this side of him, and it's unlikely they would have if he had revealed it. Aside from a few of his former girlfriends—and now his professor—no one else even knew Author Chris existed.

Chris would graduate a few weeks after our meeting, which only gave me enough time to encourage him to create at least some space in his life to write and exercise his creativity. To some extent Chris was a victim of his environment's limited capacity to understand, nurture, or appreciate creative work. Even if Chris could be a successful writer, the world he grew up in stacked the deck heavily against him even trying.

Years later, I would speak to Chris, who sounded happy, on the phone. He had been promoted multiple times at his employer, earned an MBA degree from one of the world's most prestigious universities, and made a very comfortable living. But I hadn't for-gotten our last conversation, years ago.

"Whatever happened to your writing? Did you write any short stories or a book?" I asked. After a few seconds of uncomfortable silence, his lighthearted tone abruptly changed, as if I had brought up a topic that was taboo in our friendly conversation.

"No. I thought about it a few times, but...no, I didn't. I thought about joining a writer's group to help me get started, but even if I did write a book, I thought the chances of me getting published or anyone reading it were too low to be worth it. Writing is a significant investment, and it wasn't worth the risk," he said. I realized he probably hadn't been asked this question in years, since few people knew he even had this interest. His tone remained more distant and somber for the rest of our conversation, and I realized I had touched on a painful subject. As impressive as his accomplishments had been, they had failed to satisfy the author in him.

James and the Upside

Another student of mine, James, struck me as the exact opposite of Chris when he was considering what to do for work. When he stopped by my office, he had just run directly from the campus gym to avoid being late, and was still out of breath when he sat down. Having just won the victory of showing up on time for our meeting, he began to speak. He had stopped by to get my opinion about a startup he wanted to join after graduation. The company was only a year old, but they had a good idea that had potential. He had been offered barely enough money to live, but this didn't bother him at all since he saw the potential "upside" as great. But I knew the chances of his startup succeeding, or even surviving, in a few years was questionable at best, especially given the industry they were in and how fierce the competition was. There would be few winners in the end, and it was impossible to know whether James' employer would be one of them. None of this concerned him much, despite hearing my frank assessment. The idea of having significant responsibility in an organization whose goal he was excited about, especially at his young age, was enough to attract him. He had also gotten a job offer from a consulting firm that offered over three times the compensation of the startup and a much more predictable career path, but already decided to decline. Aside from my evaluation of the startup, the only thing he had come for was advice on how best to handle declining the consulting offer he'd received.

"I want to be as nice as I can," he said. "I've never had to turn down a job offer before."

"How sure are you that you want to do this?" I asked. "You have at least a couple more weeks before you have to tell them your decision." Usually, I didn't feel the need to encourage my students to be more cautious, but James seemed especially cavalier in the way he approached his decision.

"Yes, I'm sure. There's no point in waiting a couple more weeks to tell them what I already know," he said.

He turned down the consulting firm's offer soon after our meeting, and upon graduation spent two years working for the startup that excited him so much. I'd love to tell you it became a resounding success. It didn't. Later, I would learn there were multiple existential challenges they faced even during his first months there, the sum of which would eventually lead to the startup failing and everyone being let go. The "upside" James had hoped for never materialized, and he returned to school to get a graduate degree.

A Matter of Perspective

You might think I'm telling you about Chris and James to illustrate an example of someone who played it safe and never quite ended up doing what they wanted, and someone who took a big risk doing what they wanted and failed. But if you talk to James, that's not how he sees it at all. From his point of view, he chose to work for the startup because it was something he knew he was excited about. He had little enthusiasm for taking the consulting offer, and knew he would never be excited about working there. His emotions had already given him a clear signal. The risk he was focused on was the *possibility of being miserable at work* (at the consulting firm), which shaped his vision. Chris was focused on a different type of risk: the *possibility of being unable to comfortably survive* (as a fiction writer).

The first important thing to understand about risk is that it's partly a matter of perspective. If you think James made the much riskier choice, it's probably because you see risk more like Chris. But you might also see Chris as someone who chose a vision that didn't fit well with his true self, and this also carries its own risk. We're not supposed to only have the perspective of either Chris or James, we're supposed to have *both*. Being miserable at work or unable to comfortably survive are not desirable in any life, so ignoring the risk of one or the other isn't a great strategy for happiness. My students had been conditioned in a business school environment, so many of them could easily see the risk of being unable to comfortably survive; very few truly appreciated the risk of being miserable. There has to be a conscious balance struck between the two when considering what we want to do with our lives, if we want to both comfortably survive *and* be happy.

Two More Rules of Risk

In addition to balancing both of the risks Chris and James focused on, there are two more rules to know regarding risk when making important life decisions with respect to work:

- You must always risk something to achieve any desired outcome.
- You must ensure physical survival.

The idea that taking at least some level of risk is necessary to get what we want in life means that being too focused on avoiding risk isn't going to lead to the life we want. Instead of an avoidance approach, we're often better off figuring out how to actively manage the risks we take as we go through life. For example, a common approach many entrepreneurial ventures take is not to plan brilliantly beforehand and expect to be right, but to expect to be wrong frequently and adapt each part of their business multiple times until they figure out how to succeed. Until they find it, they are simply running valuable experiments to learn what works and what doesn't work.[38]

The second rule might sound obvious, because ensuring physical survival is a basic component of living. But it's this rule where we often struggle. As I've mentioned before, the desire to survive led many of my students to respond with fear, which had a powerful influence on what they believed they could do with their lives. Many remained stuck in their jobs, miserable but feeling like they had no other choice. To some degree, this is an understandable response because the risk of being unable to survive cannot be precisely measured. We know it's there, but we can't see it clearly enough to assess exactly how dangerous it really is. And it's this uncertainty that can easily lead to a fearful response, and to bias us toward remaining stuck. We may not be living anywhere near our potential if we are stuck, but at least we're still breathing.

I don't want to sound dismissive—ensuring physical survival is important. In order to be happy and successful, we must also survive. I'm also not advocating reckless behavior. If being too focused on avoiding risk doesn't lead to the life we want, completely disregarding risk in our decisions won't either. But at least for my students, I observed that not only did they almost never have any true risk of being unable to physically survive, many of them also didn't have a significant risk of being unable to *comfortably* survive, at least for a very long time. Many were able to return home to live with their families for a while if needed, and many of my graduate students had saved enough money to live without a job for many months, if not longer. But the risks they often saw in their mind didn't reflect this at all. What they saw was something much larger and more frightening than what was really there.

Visions Are Shaped by Risk

While choosing the right vision for us is about creating alignment with our true self and not about picking a more or less risky road, the risks we see and how we respond to them will influence what our vision looks like. Because so many aspects of our education system discourage the type of risk-taking and experimentation that would have helped us become comfortable living in a world of risk, most of us are biased to avoid any significant risks we see as a product of our conditioning. I've met many people with visions much smaller than even their obviously visible potential because of their approach to risk—I know you have, too. If you want to know if this describes you, ask yourself if the vision you've created would change significantly if the world had no risk at all, if there was no possibility of any downside. If it does, your true self may want to do much more than you have planned.

For many of my students, even beyond their fears, moments of courage, and beliefs about risk, I noticed there was another obstacle—many didn't know their true selves. Not only did they not know the story of their life, they also couldn't clearly see who they were. Courage in the face of fear and managing risk would be of little help if they remained blind. Even if they weren't limited in their knowledge of the external world, the many years of education and conditioning from society were remarkably effective in limiting their awareness of who they were. This was entirely understandable. What course did you take in school that was dedicated to learning about *you*? Before we create our own visions, we must first begin to understand who we really are. It's the only way to be sure the visions we create truly align with us.

16

WHO ARE YOU, REALLY?

The privilege of a lifetime is being who you are.
~ Joseph Campbell

By nature's design, every one of us is a highly unique sentient being in the world. If our uniqueness is not an accident, then one could argue we are meant to find a way to express it in our lives. However, our society wasn't built to fully support either the exploration or expression of our individuality. This creates a fundamental challenge faced by every human being on Earth. We must somehow deal with the dilemma of how to understand and express our individual uniqueness in a world that was not exactly designed to truly understand or appreciate us.

One question I often asked the students who visited my office was why they were interested in the jobs they wanted. But this wasn't exactly what I wanted to know. What I really wanted to know was who their true self was, and what made them unique as individuals. But it was too awkward to ask them directly "Who are you, really?" and the question was too difficult to comprehend if one had never reflected on it. And because of how our education system had conditioned them, I realized many of them didn't really believe they were unique. I knew this was wrong, and I could already see parts of their individuality reveal themselves as I came to know them better. But *they* had to see it to know who they really were. How could they?

Figuring out who we are with true clarity is not something that happens in a day, or even a year. When we are young, there is usually too little information at first to know who we really are. This is because what makes us unique includes aspects of ourselves that often don't fully develop until well into adulthood. These are not things one can really know about themselves until they have accumulated enough life experiences. Even as we get older, at no point do we understand everything about who we are; we simply get a better idea if we are consciously paying attention. This is complicated further by the fact that we can change over time, even as adults. Even if we don't grow any taller, we may be continuously expanding our understanding and awareness, as long as we haven't taken a passive approach to life.

Part One of the Puzzle:
What We Enjoy, and What We Don't Enjoy

Understanding who you are to find purpose in your working life is like solving a puzzle, where you must first identify the pieces you're able to see, then begin putting them together. Because you don't see all the pieces in the beginning, an essential part of the process is making sure you're conscious enough to notice the additional pieces when life experiences reveal them. As the pieces come together, a picture will start to form. That picture is the real you. It's not defined by your external appearance, society's values, the opinions of others, or the persona you must maintain in order to operate in the outside world. If you have no idea what I mean, as a starting point take out a piece of paper and write down things you enjoy doing and things you don't enjoy doing as two separate lists next to each other. They can come from jobs, hobbies, or include any other activities. The point here is to raise awareness of what you personally enjoy, because these are the initial clues about who you are and what you were meant to do. This exercise appears deceptively simple; creating an accurate and comprehensive list can only be done by those who truly know themselves well. I've had otherwise brilliant students struggle to list more than just a couple things, then ask for my help.

As an example, below are some items from my two lists:

THINGS I ENJOY DOING

- Helping others deal with career and life challenges (surprise, surprise—I did this for years for friends and acquaintances, but didn't realize it was a signal until much later)
- Public speaking (not initially, but this came with lots of practice)
- Teaching
- Learning new ideas that change the way I think (this comes from a variety of activities, including watching lectures and reading books)
- Getting to know people from different countries/cultures
- Spending time in creative spaces (e.g., art galleries, film festivals, museums)
- Running

THINGS I DON'T ENJOY DOING
- Sitting in meetings (a required activity in most bureaucracies)
- Writing e-mails (I could be writing books instead)
- Selling products/services to others that I don't believe in (I tried telemarketing in high school and quit after I called the wife of someone who had just passed away to sell her accounting software)
- Drinking alcohol (I'm going to get into trouble for listing this one because so many social interactions have required that I do this, but I'm actually mildly allergic to alcohol)

Make sure you're honest with yourself, because it's easy to deceive ourselves into thinking we enjoy something either because the universe has rewarded us for it or not enjoying it would disappoint someone else. To make sure you're being honest, come back to your list at least one day later and consider how confident you are in your answers, that you really have answered what *you* enjoy. Also, try to be as specific as needed to be precise. For example, while many of my students said they enjoyed solving quantitative problems with data, some specifically meant doing financial statement analysis, while others meant using algorithms for prediction; they rarely enjoyed doing both. If at this point you still don't know what you enjoy or if you're struggling to write more than a couple things down, that's ok, it just means you haven't given it much conscious thought before, or you need more life experiences. There is no shame in either. As I said, we aren't encouraged much to do this, so the first attempt can feel a little awkward.

The more you write, the more puzzle pieces you will have. If you put the paper aside and come back to it later, you'll find you have more to add. You may need a bigger piece of paper. As you have more experiences in life, you will collect more puzzle pieces. But you'll need to do this consciously, otherwise you'll miss how much clearer the picture is becoming. The easiest way to do this is to write down new discoveries of what you enjoy and don't enjoy as the new information comes in. Two things will happen as you continue to do this. The first is that you will gain a much better understanding of *why* you enjoy the things you do, as well as the things you don't. The feeling of enjoying or not enjoying isn't enough to know what exactly is happening, because the emotion by itself doesn't reveal enough without more conscious thought. Writing these down will automatically focus the conscious energy needed to clarify the emotions you're feeling. The second thing that will happen is, as you continue to add new things to the list, you will start to notice a pattern. There will be common traits across different things you enjoy, as well as the things you don't enjoy. It's hard to overstate how significant this is. This is a moment when you can actually see something about yourself that's not distorted by society or anyone else.

There is a caveat to this exercise, which you have to keep in mind if you don't want to reach the wrong conclusion. The picture that comes together from the puzzle pieces I'm referring to, that's the version of you if you had no fear and didn't care about how challenging the different roads ahead in life might be. It's the picture of you if you were fearless. However, you may write things you don't enjoy on the list because they genuinely scare you, perhaps because your experiences doing those things before were painful. These fears are completely understandable. But this is the wrong starting point to understand who you really are, because using fear as a guide will naturally lead you to safer roads, which are often the roads created by others to serve something other than your true self. When looking at the list of things you don't enjoy, are any of them driven by fear, or do they all stem from a genuine lack of enjoyment? Or, to put it another way, if you weren't afraid at all while doing these things, do you think you might actually enjoy them? Here, the most reliable items on the list are the things that are not associated with fear, or where fear is not the main cause of not enjoying them. The different challenges associated with choosing different paths in life are important considerations, but not at the very beginning, when you're just trying to understand who you are.

Part Two of the Puzzle: Our Values

Each one of us has a unique combination of values—it's a critical part of who we are. In our working life, they serve as a sign telling us how we might feel when doing particular activities or when in certain environments. Some of my students had values that didn't align well with a business school environment and were some of the most miserable students I ever had, even if their performance in class was outstanding. Our values matter tremendously in determining what paths are the right ones for us in life.

There are many ways to begin exploring our values. One simple way to start is to remove any constraints from your beliefs about reality and visualize what a perfect working life would look like for yourself. Forget about what you think is possible or realistic. Instead, imagine you already have as much money as you could ever want, what other people think is completely irrelevant, and just focus on what you would ideally want to be doing with your life. Visualize it in as much detail as you can, and write down everything you see.

- What are you doing exactly, and why does it matter to you?
- Where are you doing the work, and why does it feel good to be there?
- Is the work environment highly structured and predictable, or is it fluid and unpredictable?
- Are you working together with others, or are you working alone?
- If there are others, what's your working relationship with them like, and how would you describe their character and values?

The scenes that emerge in your mind will provide a number of answers about what your values are. For example, if you want to know if you value autonomy above security, the scenes you see will reveal the answer. These questions sound simple, but answering them fully is not. What you see in the beginning will only capture what's on the surface, but if you continue watching the scenes in your mind consciously you will see more and more detail, all of which provide clues to your values. And similar to creating the list of things you do or don't enjoy, you might struggle with this at first because you may be giving conscious thought to something that has never been cultivated before, or need more life experiences to see the scenes more clearly. Give it time, and don't give up. The scenes will become clearer.

Another way of doing this exercise is to consider what the perfect working life would be for someone else you know, but which you feel would be very unappealing for yourself. Why do you find their version so unattractive? Whichever way you do this exercise, you'll find that what comes out may be closely related to or even overlap with the list of things you enjoy and don't enjoy. This is natural and should come as no surprise—these pieces are all meant to fit together to create the same picture of who you are.

Similar to the previous exercise, a caveat exists to doing this one, too. If you're imagining the perfect working life for yourself is not to be working at all, this isn't the right answer. Many people, especially those who are miserable in the jobs they do, believe work is fundamentally unpleasant, painful, and without real purpose or meaning. In this view of the world, the highest quality of life one can achieve is to not work at all and pursue a life of leisure. Or at least, that's the theory. This belief is so common it actually serves as a powerful incentive for many, where they count down the years of their lives until they can retire, although this usually means they must sacrifice the vast majority of their finite lives feeling miserable and empty before they get there. But the point of this exercise is to explore what work aligns more closely with your values to improve how you feel in your working life, not to dream of not working at all. Visualizing what this looks like is an important first step.

Putting the different pieces of the puzzle together sounds very easy to do, and it is in principle, if one keeps working at it. It's also something I hardly ever see anyone do. The reality is, most of us never put enough of the pieces together to see who we really are with real clarity. If we did, knowing the story of our life and creating visions would be much easier. But at best, we often only have a vague idea of who we are, even though signals in life have told us much more than we've noticed. I frequently saw evidence of this with the students who visited my office, where I could see pieces of their puzzle that fit together, but they hadn't yet put them together. This was no stroke of genius on my part; they could have seen it easily for themselves, if they had done the con-

scious work. The more clearly they could see the picture of themselves, the more confidence they would have in moving forward
in their lives, and in finding purpose. But where did purpose fit in
with their other needs?

17

OUR NEED FOR PURPOSE

If you deliberately plan to be less than you are capable of being, then I warn you that you'll be deeply unhappy for the rest of your life.
~ Abraham Maslow

What do we really need in life? This question may sound heavy and philosophical, but it's one of the most important questions we can ask as human beings. If we understand what our needs are, we can work to make sure they are provided for. If we don't understand what they are, we risk feeling empty and unful-filled but never truly knowing why. Because of this, there is immense practical value for the quality of our lives if we know the answer and can keep it in our conscious mind. We can also more clearly understand why we need purpose, and where it fits relative to our other needs. So, where do we begin to find the answer?

Maslow's Hierarchy of Needs

In the mid-twentieth century, a psychologist named Abraham Maslow dedicated his life to researching what the answer might be. While many in the field of psychology were concerned with studying the causes of dysfunctional behavior and mental illness, Maslow was interested in understanding the potential human beings had to live happy and fulfilling lives as individuals. How were humans able to do this, and what did this look like? In his search for an answer, he began to study what people needed in life to reach their potential, and identified what he believed were universal needs every individual had. These needs could be represented as a hierarchy, which is presented here:[39]

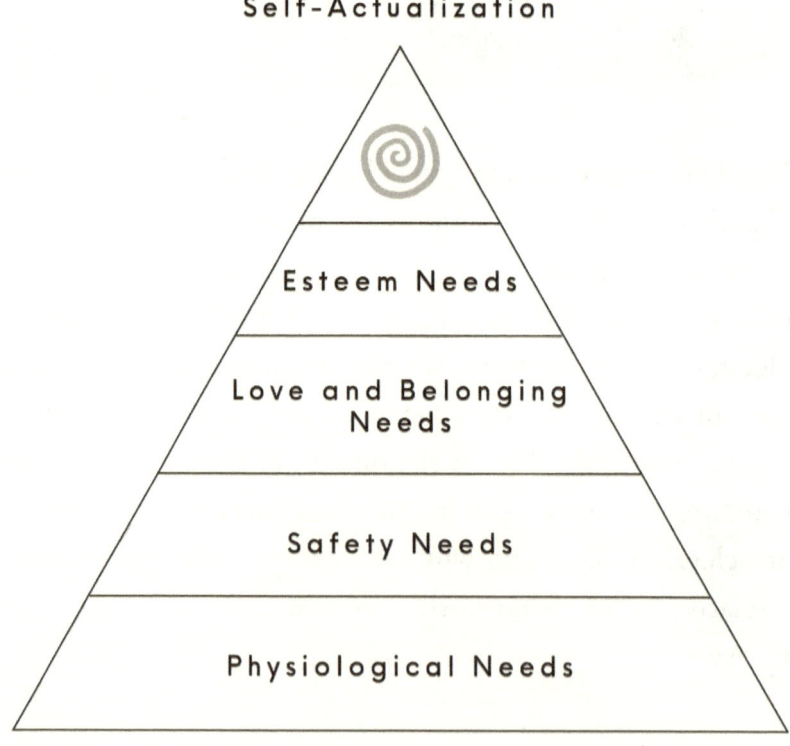

As you can see from the pyramid, at the bottom are our physiological needs, which include food, water, and shelter. They are the most basic things we need to survive. Our safety needs include security and protection, both physically as well as psychologically. We may be surviving every day if our physiological needs are met, but we cannot have a high quality of life if we're constantly feeling unsafe. The third level represents our need for love and belonging, which we find through human connections including family, friendships, and intimate relationships with others. The fourth level, our esteem needs, refers to our need for status, recognition, attention, a sense of confidence, and a belief in one's ability to achieve. At the top of the pyramid is what Maslow referred to as self-actualization, which is the desire to manifest our full potential as individuals. This is where our need for purpose primarily comes from, if it is an expression of our true self.

If these are our universal human needs, then it's worth considering for a moment how well we're doing at meeting all of them. If you look at the pyramid, where are you satisfied today, and where are you not satisfied? Assessing this isn't something we can do with our rational mind. Not having our needs met is something we understand by sensing it. We know when we are hungry or feel unsafe. We know when we aren't satisfied with what we've achieved. But understanding our progress with meeting *all* our different needs, especially our need for self-actualization, requires a sufficient level of consciousness.

Being Conscious Enough to Evaluate Our Needs

Physiological and safety needs don't require much self-awareness in order to be evaluated. Your body tells you clearly when you are hungry, and you can easily recognize when your brain tells you you're not safe. These are needs we have accumulated a considerable amount of experience with from a very young age, so we're very familiar with them. The need for status, recognition, and achievement is also typically straightforward to assess because the goals we set and the competitions we enter in our society are usually structured to provide clear feedback. Our evaluation of ourselves, which includes our beliefs about how worthy and capable we are, is also something we can easily know, although the answer may not be comfortable to acknowledge. However, assessing how well we're meeting our need for human connection, especially love, is not as straightforward because it requires knowing what these connections should look and feel like. If someone does not know what a healthy, loving relationship looks like and has never experienced it before, how can they accurately tell if they are in such a relationship now? It's still possible to know, but it doesn't come from an immediate, familiar sense of knowing. It has to be learned. It might seem we should naturally know this the same way our hunger tells us we need to eat, but this is far from reality. Individuals who unknowingly starve for lack of food are rare, but in our society, it's all too common to see those lacking enough human connection who do not fully appreciate they are, in fact, starving.

Out of all the universal needs Maslow proposed, our need for self-actualization requires the most consciousness. We really need to know ourselves well to experience it, because it's about expressing our true selves. This is more difficult than it sounds. The demands and expectations of society and those around us can work so strongly to suppress our true selves that we may have no idea what *self*-actualization even means. We may also have chosen to compromise or hide important parts of ourselves in order to meet our other needs, which can become a powerful obstacle. Moreover, there is no universal answer for what self-actualization looks like, because each of us is so unique. Meeting the need for self-actualization can look radically different across individuals, to a much larger degree than any of the other needs Maslow identified. We may all have a similar idea of what it means to be physically safe, to the point where we may even be able to learn how to be safe by observing others, but imitating the exact path of someone else who has experienced self-actualization can easily lead to a life of meaningless misery. But this is no reason for despair, only a reason why we need to become more aware of who we really are.

How does one assess whether their needs for human connection and self-actualization are being satisfied? It isn't enough to simply not feel empty or unhappy, because this information alone doesn't quite provide the full picture. Collecting many life experiences is also not sufficient by itself. One must be conscious enough to see what's happening. If the experiences we have in life are part of a movie we are starring in, then our level of consciousness is the lens through which we see both what's happening around us as well as inside of us. Our lens may be wide, allowing us to see more of what's taking place, or it may be narrow, and we may only be able to see a small part of the events unfolding. Our lens may be focused only on what's right in front of us, but may be unable to focus on anything happening even slightly further away. We need a lens that allows us to see a wide view of our reality, and to be able to focus clearly on what's happening both inside us as well as off in the distance. None of this is beyond our ability; it only requires combining the regular practice of self-reflection with the gathering of enough life experiences, which brings awareness to the lens and how to control it to see life more clearly. To the uninitiated this may sound overly simplistic or difficult to believe, but this is a natural part of our ability to sense the progression of our lives, if only we would practice paying a little more attention. If we can see, then we will know.

Our Society's Unbalanced Approach to Our Needs

If you don't feel like you've experienced self-actualization before or have trouble understanding what it even means, you're not alone. During his research, Maslow found very few people experienced it. Self-actualization highlights an important challenge we all face to experience something that can remain elusive for our entire lives. Our society is also not designed to help individuals achieve self-actualization. If you listen to what political leaders in our society discuss as their main concerns, they are predominantly physiological and safety needs, and to some extent esteem needs. People need to have enough to eat every day for their survival, and to feel physically safe. They also need ways to gain status and recognition, and to be rewarded for achieving something. As a result of our society's narrow focus on these particular needs, much of the rhetoric we hear from many in government is about jobs. Jobs must be provided, especially those that pay well enough with opportunities for even higher pay and status in the future. No one should be taking these jobs away from us. We also hear promises that any threats to our safety will be decisively addressed, whether they be in our communities or from abroad. By contrast, few politicians speak about addressing the need for human connection, or the need to help every individual experience self-actualization. It just isn't in the design. This unbalanced focus of our society's design leads to predictably unbalanced outcomes: a significant number of people who lack close human connection, and only a small number of people who experience self-actualization.[40]

Our need for self-actualization comes from a much deeper, existential place within us compared to our other needs. It's a need to express the story of our life and visions we create, to provide a meaningful confirmation of why we are here. It validates our uniqueness in a way that eating, feeling safe, having status and recognition, and even being loved cannot. So few things in life acknowledge or appreciate our individuality to this degree that self-actualization is often considered a profound life experience, even spiritual in nature. And why wouldn't it be? One has experienced life at their full potential as a human being.

Meeting our need for self-actualization, the expression of our true self, requires having enough knowledge, courage, and consciousness. This is how we find our sense of purpose. It's a much more challenging and less obvious road than meeting any of our other human needs. In this sense, it's the most demanding of all of our needs, but also our highest calling as we go through life. Finding the way requires knowledge that comes from experience, which we must see with the lens of our consciousness in focus. But what kind of experiences can tell us what our purpose might be, what the right vision is for us? Surprisingly, an answer can come from experiences that bring us significant, often transformative, emotional pain.

18

FROM PAIN TO PURPOSE

There is no normal life that is free of pain. It's the very wrestling with our problems that can be the impetus for our growth.
~ Mister Rogers

Given how little we learn in school about our emotions, it should come as no surprise many people struggle to understand or deal with emotional pain. By contrast, we have a very good sense of how to react when we experience physical pain. If we break our arm or leg, we know to visit a doctor quickly and get treatment. Afterward, we take care of our body until the injury is healed. Ignoring the injury would make little sense. But if we experience emotional pain, we may be much less likely to respond with the same urgency or degree of self-care, and may even avoid seeking treatment because we feel too embarrassed to acknowledge we are injured. Biologically however, we feel emotional pain in a very similar way that we feel physical pain.[41] The pain of being psychologically traumatized, rejected, or heartbroken is just as real as the pain from physical injury. But unlike physical pain, a much wider range of possibilities can occur.

The Meaning of Emotionally Painful Experiences

One of the most striking characteristics of humans is how different our responses are to the same emotionally painful experience. As much as we may all be similar, this demonstrates we're also remarkably different. Every day humanity struggles with emotional pain, which can come from experiences including failure, rejection, health issues, the ending of a relationship, the loss of a loved one, or an injustice of some kind. Though we may prefer to avoid these experiences, they are a fundamental part of life itself. Many of these experiences occur due to factors that are out of our control, which means we may not be able to directly "fix" the cause of our emotional pain the moment we experience it. This often makes the pain feel more intense. But it's what we say the moment we're in pain that defines what happens next. And we do not, despite the similarity in what we feel, all say the same thing.

One reason why we don't all react the same way to emotional pain is because the universe doesn't often provide a good answer for why painful experiences occur. We may know the immediate cause of the experience, but this answer can be unsatisfying because we may feel surely there must be a better, more profound reason that such bad things happen. However, if such an objective reason does exist, life appears fundamentally designed for us not to know what it is. We are left to make sense of the pain on our own. Our starting point for doing this is our philosophy of life, and our core beliefs about ourselves.

Our philosophy of life, our theory of how life works, helps us to understand all the events we experience, including those that bring pain. For example, our theory may include a belief that the universe is generally helping us to achieve what we want. If we are then passed over for a promotion at work due to someone else's unjust decision, it may seem logical to conclude our experience is not what would normally occur, and that we have an opportunity to make another attempt that would lead to a better outcome. The system we are part of may not always work the way it should, but we may believe it will eventually work. But if we believe the universe is working against us, it may be logical to conclude we are being held back by a more powerful and systemic force, and making another attempt would likely result in the same painful experience again.

In addition to our philosophy of life, our core beliefs about ourselves—the beliefs that begin to form starting early in our lives, which answer important questions about ourselves—will also create our understanding of what we experience.

- Am I capable?
- Am I good enough?
- Do people like me?

If we have positive experiences early on that provide only encouraging answers to these questions, we are off to a great start in life because we will already have evidence that confirms positive beliefs. With enough positive answers, we will naturally begin to adopt a positive set of core beliefs about ourselves. However, if our experiences are negative and we are given discouraging answers, they will often lead to the adoption of negative beliefs. Similarly, these negative beliefs will begin to construct a much darker understanding of ourselves. A common belief for those who form this darker understanding is that they are not worthy of good things happening to them in life. No one is born believing this, but many are told this implicitly or explicitly when they are young. If we have this as a core belief and experience rejection, it may seem logical to conclude the rejection confirms our lack of worth. Core beliefs can change as we have new experiences, but only if they lead to a new understanding.

Our philosophy of life and core beliefs about ourselves come together to create a basic understanding of what happens to us throughout life. This is especially true in moments of intense emotional pain. Using the examples mentioned earlier, our theory of how life works may include the belief that the universe is working against us, and that we are not worthy of good things happening to us in life. If we are then passed over for a promotion, we may be more likely to conclude the rejection is still a valid signal of our worth. It's difficult to deny the pain of rejection, which feels much more intense if we define our worth based on the evaluations of others. We may then choose to quit pursuing what led to our rejection any further because we believe the universe is too strong a force to overcome, and we may also become more passive in our approach to living. However, if we instead believe the universe is generally helping us to achieve what we want and that we are capable of accomplishing anything we desire, then we may interpret our experience as a temporary setback on the road to a successful outcome, albeit a painful one. Given this understanding, we may then choose to persist on our current path, believing success will eventually come. In each case, the same painful experience has occurred, but results in the opposite response.

Purpose Born from Pain

How does pain lead to purpose, then? Our basic understanding of an emotionally painful event may come from our philosophy of life and core beliefs about ourselves, but this alone does not lead to discovering a sense of purpose. A painful experience must also lead to a profound shift in the way we see something in us and in the world. We must become aware of something we did not know before. It may be as simple as realizing how painful an experience is for everyone who goes through it, which we did not truly understand until we experienced it for ourselves. For example, it's difficult to comprehend what having a life-threatening illness or losing a loved one feels like unless we've also had the same experience. Or, if we experience social injustice, the painful experience may press strongly upon our values, where we realize they have been severely violated. Knowing that others also suffer from the same injustice can trigger a strong reaction inside us that we cannot easily brush aside. In each of these cases, the experience of emotional pain adds a perspective we may not have had otherwise.

Once our perspective has changed and we have a basic interpretation of the emotional pain we feel, we have one final piece to consider: Is there enough motive for action? The action may be either for us or for others, but in each case, aims to diminish the emotional pain. Each of us must determine whether our threshold for taking action has been crossed. The threshold is defined by a series of questions. Should I do something about it? Am I able to make a difference? Can I accept this happening to others without doing something? Am I willing to bear the cost of taking action? Is now the right time to do something? If we have sufficient motive to take action, the words we use in our answers will indicate this. I *must* do something about it. I *can* make a difference. I *cannot* accept this happening to others. I *am* willing to bear the cost of taking action. Something needs to be done *now*.

We may also have individual characteristics that increase the chances we will take action. If we have more empathy for others, we will have greater motivation to help others deal with or avoid the same painful experience. If we have a strong sense of moral justice and the cause of our emotional pain violates this, we may find it unacceptable to let the injustice continue without trying to address it. We may also realize the skills we have are both useful and necessary to deal with the cause of the painful experience, and there is no one better than us who has emerged to deal with it. Our painful experience may, unexpectedly, pull on something that's part of our unique identity.

If we take action, we bring our own meaning to the emotional pain, which might otherwise have been seen as meaningless. This is an exercise of one of the most powerful abilities we have as human beings. We take something painful that has happened and, unsatisfied with the universe's silence in answering the question of "Why did this happen to me?" we create our own more satisfying answer. If others see what we're doing, we may discover they wish to join us in taking action because we've changed their perspective, and they also have enough motive for action. This may manifest in something as straightforward as the gathering of people to share their experiences, to realize they are not alone in their suffering. These collective gatherings may also lead to greater awareness of how to deal with these painful experiences. In some cases, an organized effort may emerge to directly cope with or eliminate the cause of the emotional pain for others. In time, we may find our decision to take action led to a vision that, in a strange way, gave us a much stronger sense of purpose than we ever had before. We may also find our negative core beliefs about ourselves, which might have seemed to be an undeniable truth, begin to fade away as we evolve to become someone different.

One might argue that bringing one's own meaning to an emotionally painful experience is not truly real. From this point of view, events occur for clear and objective reasons we can observe, and any attempt to create more meaning is a disingenuous way to deal with the pain. Nothing could be further from the truth. What gives life meaning is nothing more than the fact that we see it as meaningful. Meaning is a matter of what we believe, not what we see with our own eyes or what we can prove. If others join us in taking action to deal with emotional pain, it's not because we have been so effective at proving something to be true; it's because they believe the same thing we do. Our ability to believe things we cannot see or prove in our immediate circumstances is an essential part of how humanity has accomplished its biggest triumphs. It gives us power when in every other way we may feel powerless. The person who loses a loved one to a disease may believe they must work to prevent or cure it in others, even though no one has told them to do so. One who has experienced a social injustice may believe they must create a movement for change, and work to create a better world for all of us. In the moment we experience emotional pain, we struggle to make sense of what's happened and what we see with our conscious lens may expand. Out of this struggle, we may find meaning that leads to a purposeful vision, and manifest it by taking action. This is one of the most real things we do as human beings.

19

FROM FLOW TO PURPOSE

*In our studies, we found that every flow activity, whether
it involved competition, chance, or any other dimension of
experience, had this in common: It provided a sense of discovery,
a creative feeling of transporting the person into a new reality.*
~ Mihaly Csikszentmihalyi

Early in my career as a professor, I attended an event where a panel
of distinguished entrepreneurs had come to campus to share their
personal stories of success and failure with a large auditorium full
of undergraduate students. When members of the audience were
given the opportunity to ask questions at the end, one student
eagerly approached the microphone and asked the panel what
they believed the key to their success was, in one sentence. After
a brief pause, the first three panelists gave the same answer: "Do
what you love." The fourth panelist, seeing the excitement gradually fade on the student's face with each additional response, said:
"Never be afraid of failure." I could sense dissatisfaction through-

out the room. It was as if they had been told a secret they wanted to know would remain out of reach.

The advice to *do what you love* is so commonly offered it has become an unsatisfying cliché to many, to the point where one may choose to mention a more surprising pearl of wisdom to avoid disappointing their audience. This reflects an unfair expectation often placed on those who are asked for such advice, which presumes they must have a well-kept secret that explains their success, which would change the lives of others if only they would be generous enough to share it. Although it may be tempting to believe this is true, there is no secret, at least not in the way we might expect. It turns out that when we do something we love, very often it's not only that our enjoyment gives us more energy to accomplish our goals; we also spend much more of our time in a different, extraordinary state of mind.

Our Extraordinary Superpower

The exceptional state of mind we may experience is what psychologist Mihaly Csikszentmihalyi referred to as being in *flow*.[42] Being in flow is when you are completely immersed in what you're doing. You are performing at your best, and you know this not intellectually, but because you *feel* it. Your actions don't feel forced, but come automatically, even effortlessly. You feel a sense of absolute clarity about what you're doing, along with the confidence you can do it successfully. There is no sense of panic or anxiety, and the critical voice in your head fades away along with other distractions, replaced by a sense of calm and connection to the task at hand. You lose track of time, or more precisely, your sense of time. When in flow, doing the activity is its own reward.

It's not about the money, recognition, or whatever else the external world provides for doing it. Being in flow is nothing less than a radically different state of existence, a different way of experiencing life, which occurs when we're at our peak performance as human beings.

What does someone in flow look like? Common examples we might see in public are when elite athletes, chess players, artists, musicians, actors, and dancers perform at their best. In less-public settings, doctors may be in flow when doing surgery. Computer programmers may be riveted to their keyboards, coding with complete and total focus. Even business managers have reported being in flow. In a ten-year study conducted by the global consulting firm McKinsey & Company, executives working while in flow reported being 500% more productive.[43] That's the power of *five* of you going to work in the morning when you're not in flow. The difference in comparison to our more mundane state of mind isn't even close. Flow is a version of ourselves we might think of as superhuman, or perhaps even superhero, except all humans have the potential to experience it. Under the right conditions, we really can go from being ordinary to extraordinary.[44]

If you haven't had many experiences being in flow, there's nothing wrong with you. It's largely a result of the environments you've been in your entire life, and the activities you've spent your time doing. For many who go through our society's education system, there is little to no understanding or experience of being in flow. This is because the system itself doesn't explicitly recognize flow.[45] It may never tell students about its importance, or specifically seek to guide them to experience it for themselves. Flow is hard to measure, and what induces it is highly unique to each individual. These are exactly the kinds of characteristics that create headaches for a bureaucracy, and therefore create powerful incentives for a bureaucracy to ignore it. What's strongly preferred is something much easier to measure, something that doesn't need to consider the possibility that everyone is truly different and, under their own unique conditions, can demonstrate exceptional performance. It should be no surprise, then, that the use of standardized tests remains immensely popular among educational bureaucracies throughout the world. But this does little to help students understand what puts them in flow. And flow is our state of extraordinary peak performance.

With few exceptions, employers are also not well-suited to fostering flow, despite the incredible productivity increases that would result if only they were. Again, much of this is due to the nature of bureaucracies, which by design prefer standardized rules and norms over recognizing individuals as having unique needs that, if met, would likely lead to much higher performance. The preference for standardization and regulation runs deep within most organizations because it gives bureaucracies the power to control their members, theoretically for the good of the organization. The larger an organization grows, the more necessary such control becomes to efficiently coordinate everyone who is part of it. A perennial belief also exists among the management of many bureaucracies that their organization can be improved by creating more rules and policies, even if they possess only a limited understanding of the true consequences of their actions for others who work in the organization. For some managers, this approach is especially appealing because it aligns with their personal view that controlling others leads to better outcomes instead of granting greater autonomy. Unfortunately, none of this helps human beings enter flow, and almost always generates distractions and obstacles when trying to create the required conditions.

Despite all this, it's still possible to experience being in flow in our lives. While we are all unique in terms of what specific activities and environments lead us to experience it, several common characteristics are present across all of them.

1. The activity needs to be challenging to the point where it demands complete focus, but not so challenging we become too frustrated while doing it.
2. There must also be a clearly defined goal we're working toward when doing the activity, coupled with regular feedback about how we're doing.
3. Unproductive distractions must be minimized, because we cannot experience flow when we're distracted.
4. We also need a sense of autonomy when we do the activity—being micromanaged by someone else while engaged in an activity can destroy our ability to experience flow.
5. It helps if you do what you love, or at the very least, enjoy.

Flow as a Signal of Purpose

Flow can be an important signal pointing to the type of work that might give us a sense of purpose for two reasons.

First, if you're able to spend more of your time in flow while doing an activity, you have an enormous advantage in getting better at it. The more you experience flow, the more you are at your peak performance. It really is you at your very best, when you're doing something amazing. The more hours, days, and months you spend in this state, what you can accomplish multiplies well beyond what you could do in the same amount of time without experiencing flow. If we demonstrate such power so easily when doing an activity, it becomes natural to consider whether the activity may have relevance for our purpose.

Second, being in flow is often an element of experiencing a significantly higher quality of life with purpose—a life that includes genuine happiness. This was one of Csikszentmihalyi's most significant discoveries during his research. When asked to recall the happiest moments of their lives, the people he interviewed didn't mention blessings that fell from the sky, having money, or sitting idle on a beach. They came from circumstances when they chose to push their mental or physical limits to accomplish something difficult and meaningful. And during these experiences, they described being in a completely different state of mind—the feeling of being in flow.[46] Flow can be a sign of what may give us a sense of purpose, and lead us to greater happiness and satisfaction in our working lives.

For some, being aware of the importance of flow is already enough to find the type of work that provides a sense of purpose. However, for most of us, awareness alone is not enough. One common problem that arises is we may not experience flow frequently enough in our life for it to be a useful positive signal, although the lack of it is often itself a revealing negative signal. This dilemma may arise from not doing enough of what we already know induces flow for us. This may sound like an easy problem to solve, and intellectually it is: Do work that includes more of what you already know puts you in flow. But as I observed with many of my students, the human mind can create an astonishing number of reasons for why doing more of what induces flow is simply not possible, or even desirable. This is a tragically self-destructive way of approaching the problem, when the mind should really be focused on answering "How do I do more of what puts me in flow?"

Another reason why we may not have enough flow experiences is because we haven't tried a wide enough variety of activities. One semester, I asked all of my classes whether they had experienced being in flow at school or work within the last week. In my undergraduate class, a considerable number of hands went up. In my part-time MBA course, which consisted mainly of older, working professionals who had full-time jobs, only one hand went up. I discovered my undergraduate class had many more experiences with flow in part because they were doing a much wider range of different activities. All of them were simultaneously learning various subjects in their other courses, and many had chosen to take classes covering topics they were genuinely interested in. Many were also engaged in other club activities at school or various pet projects. By contrast, many of my older students had become competent at a much narrower set of activities over time but were not operating at the limit of their capabilities. They had stopped living in a way that allowed them to find new activities that led to experiencing flow. Regardless of age, an important part of finding purpose in life is continuing to find activities that bring us these experiences. And since modern adult life is often not structured to give us this variety without conscious effort, we must keep exploring.

One important caveat exists when considering flow as we evolve to finding our purpose: not every activity where you experience flow is necessarily something you should be doing in your working life. If you're in flow while washing dishes at home, should you quit your job and start washing dishes for a living? Maybe, but not necessarily. So, you'll need to sift through the activities where you experience being in flow. A personal sense of meaning in the activity must be present. The ones that have this, write them down. They are more pieces of the puzzle that help reveal the real picture of you. Even though not all flow experiences are signals meant to help you find a sense of purpose, successful people who work with purpose often spend much more of their time in flow. This is especially true for those who are incredibly successful. And even if we have never heard of flow before, we may instinctively stop to observe someone if we notice they are performing in flow, because we might witness them do something extraordinary. And it is extraordinary. It's like watching someone doing what they were born to do.

20

THE DISCOVERY PROCESS

The real work of our lives is to become aware.
And awakened. To answer the call.
~ Oprah Winfrey

In nature, there is a beautiful and complex system of living things all working together in a coordinated manner. Every plant and animal has a role to play, and behaves according to its design. In the forest, the trees do not wonder if they should grow taller, and the birds do not wonder if they should sing; they simply do what they were designed to do. For humans, life is more complicated. Beyond meeting our most basic needs, nature gives us no precise instructions about what we're supposed to be doing. At the same time, having a sense of purpose fulfills a universal human need that's part of our design. As we go through life, the experiences we have, especially those that are painful or lead us to flow, provide us with helpful signs if we're conscious enough to notice them. But even when we see the signs, purpose usually does not come automatically. It's most often the product of an intentional, structured process.

While self-reflection is an essential part of finding purpose, purpose does not come from being in isolation. It reveals itself when you engage the universe to learn about the fit between yourself and the external world. It begins with understanding your true self. Others may not see it, but you have always been there, with your own highly unique design. You face the external world, which offers many roads. These roads are the different possibilities of what you can do with the finite amount of time life gives you, all of which will present their own challenges. You will choose a road, consciously or not. A strong sense of purpose is what occurs when your true self fits with the road chosen. It's a feeling of going in the right direction, even if the exact twists and turns on the road ahead aren't yet known.

Earlier in this book, I provided some exercises to help you begin to understand who you really are. They are meant to give you different pieces of the puzzle of yourself, to begin uncovering the true picture of you. For many people, this is the first step of their evolution to purpose. It's exploring your own unique design as a human being and separating away all of the external world's expectations and implanted voices in your head. A critical key to this process is to not view it as a race, or even as something that can be successfully completed within a short period of time. Otherwise, the picture may become distorted because the desire to finish quickly will create a bias that destroys the integrity of the process. Puzzle pieces that are "maybe" become "definitely" in the interests of speed, even if they're not correct. Two pieces that would fit even better if a third piece was introduced suddenly leads to the third piece being added to create a coherent picture, even if no experience exists to support it. We are remarkably vulnerable to self-deception if it gives us a sense of accomplishment. Pieces of the puzzle must be uncovered incrementally and with care, more so than anything else we might do. What we're doing is the equivalent of looking in the mirror on a regular basis and asking what we can clearly see, and if anything has changed.

Once you see the picture of yourself begin to appear, it's time to consider what the person you see was meant to do with their life. What activities do you enjoy that also align well with your values? From the activities you wrote down earlier that you enjoy, some will resonate more strongly than others when seeing how well they fit in the context of your perfect working life. Pay close attention to those that resonate most strongly—they are the most conclusive data you have until you collect new experiences. You may even have seen yourself doing these activities already when you visualized what a perfect working life would look like for yourself. If the list seems long, rank them by how confident you feel about each one. Don't worry about whether you're doing this correctly or incorrectly. Very often this will look messy and feel awkward if one has never done it before. You are evolving from being shaped by the demands of the external world to acting intentionally from your true self. It's a little like learning how to drive for the first time.

For each activity you identify, consider whether your description would be more accurate if you were even more specific. Try to answer in detail who you're interacting with, what exactly is being done, and where you're doing it. For the activities you've chosen that originally came from imagining your perfect working life, you may have already done much of this. You can use the same technique to come up with more precise descriptions of the other activities you've added. Also, as you do this, focus more on specific activities you want to do as opposed to thinking of a particular job. Jobs usually consist of multiple activities, some of which you may enjoy and others you would prefer not to do, so mixing them together simultaneously in the beginning can muddle the process of evaluation. If you find it much easier to think of jobs instead of activities, then identify the activities within a job that fit the picture of you.

Start with Yourself First, Then Look Outside

When identifying the activities that best fit both what you enjoy and what aligns with your values, do this *before* you think about the options the universe has placed immediately in front of you. Do not think a reasonable or more efficient first step would be to see what jobs are currently out there first. If you do that, you are asking the external world what it wants right now. But the external world doesn't know you, and is much more limited in its imagination than you are. Seeing what the external world presents in front of you right now as a first step also weakens your capacity to create visions, because it gives a strong false impression that what you see in the world right now is really all there is. Doing things in this order can lead to a completely different answer about what you should ultimately do. And if you want to find purpose, it will often be the wrong answer.

Once you've identified the activities you feel confident about that fit your values best, you can begin to look at the external world. At any given moment in life, the external world will present a set of prepackaged options, the most obvious of which are job openings, each of which can be evaluated against the activities you've identified to see how well they match. But more important than these options, the external world will also show you what the building blocks are that you might be able to use to create something that fits you better. This may also take the form of jobs, but this description is too narrow. Building blocks are the relationships you develop with others, valuable knowledge you can acquire, or anything else you find in the external world that can help you. If we are unconscious with a limited view of life, all we will see are the jobs in our immediate environment and believe that's all the world offers us. But if we expand our consciousness and our foundation of knowledge, we can start to imagine what might happen if we join different combinations of the building blocks we see in the external world. The activities that fit us best serve as a guide for how we might use them. The combinations of building blocks we see in our mind construct our visions.

Four Guiding Principles for Creating Visions

While there is no universal or best way to create visions, we must follow four guiding principles before making the final decision to choose one.

The first guiding principle is to not limit your imagination at the outset. This may sound easy, but in practice it was one of the biggest challenges my students struggled with. When we're young, it's incredibly easy to imagine ourselves doing anything we put our minds to. By the time my undergraduate students came to my office, they already began to suffer from constraints to their imagination but still retained enough of its essence to see a wide range of possibilities in their future with a little help. But for many of my older students, it was incredibly difficult for them to imagine doing anything other than what they were already doing. This doesn't happen because imagination declines with age; it happens because it fades with lack of use, like any other ability we have. When creating visions, the key is to begin with as many constraints removed as possible and exercise our imagination. If our imagination is diminished, it can be revived again. Everyone has their own way of revitalizing a weakened imagination, which usually involves minimizing limiting and negative forces and replacing them with inspiring and energizing ones. One of the fastest ways to do this is to change one's environment dramatically, even if only temporarily. Getting one's imagination to work at its peak is not about putting in enough effort or having enough stamina. It's about recharging oneself and refocusing to be able to see what's been in plain sight all along.

The second guiding principle is to recognize there will often be a conflict between what we call our heart and our rational mind. The heart is grounded in our emotions, while the rational mind is our problem-solving computer. Our heart may tell us a vision is right for us, and our rational mind may tell us to run away as far and as fast as we can. The opposite can just as easily occur. Each reaches its conclusion based on different information. The heart is guided by emotional responses to both our experiences as well as the future outcome we imagine. Even if the future outcome is uncertain, it can still feel great or terrible right now if we visualize it in our minds. By contrast, the rational mind makes assumptions and analyzes the available data to make a prediction about the future outcome. The assumptions the rational mind makes come from our beliefs, and the rational mind must rely heavily on them because our experiences don't provide enough data to reach any truly reliable conclusions. Whether we realize it or not, our beliefs usually play a much larger role than any facts in weighing the pros and cons of pursuing a vision.

What do we do when our heart and mind give us different answers about whether we should pursue a vision? No universally correct answer exists, but we do need to keep a couple of things in mind. Because the rational mind isn't good at judging what would make us happier, relying on it alone as a guide can be dangerous. This does not mean our heart is always accurate, but it's at least capable of steering us in the right direction under the right conditions. Also, regardless of what vision we choose to pursue, unforeseen challenges will arise which at times will be both painful and exhausting. Our rational mind in theory can attempt to predict and evaluate these challenges in advance, but life is too uncertain and complex for us to see all of them beforehand, no matter how hard we try. What allows us to face these challenges successfully is almost never rational analysis, but having enough emotional fuel to power us forward. Following our heart increases the chances we will have enough fuel in these moments to persevere, and ultimately succeed when pursuing our vision.

The third guiding principle in choosing a vision is to be extremely selective with whom you discuss it. Over the years, I lost count of the number of students I've had who considered pursuing a vision, told someone about it, and became so discouraged from the feedback they received they threw the idea away. Some of the people they had trusted to ask enjoyed playing the role of critic with the façade of being helpful. It's an easy role to play, and can bring great satisfaction if one has convinced someone else of their wisdom. Others were genuinely well-intentioned, but harbored strong views of the world that were not shared by my students. In every case, none of the people consulted really understood who my students were as individuals. When it comes to visions, those who are genuinely helpful and supportive are not common enough in our society. Be careful who you discuss your vision with if you haven't yet decided to pursue it.

The fourth and last guiding principle is to confirm the vision carries significant meaning for you. Doing everything mentioned up until this point dramatically increases the chances that your vision has significant meaning, but in the end, you are the final judge. This cannot be evaluated accurately with your rational mind, because fundamentally, purpose is grounded in emotion and expression, not analysis or calculation. People who have a strong sense of purpose at work don't have to logically convince themselves they have purpose. They know they have it simply because they *feel* it. Answering the following can be a confirmation test: Why is the vision you have chosen so important to you? If you can answer this clearly, without struggle, and you have no difficulty believing your answer, you're on the right track.

Creating and choosing to pursue a vision is a fundamental part of expressing our unique individuality in the world. It's the most important step we can take to live life on our own terms, and not live only for the demands of the external world. If we can consciously navigate the indifferent, and at times even hostile, education system and work environments within our society to create an authentic vision that fits with our true self, this already is a remarkable accomplishment. It means we have found a true sense of purpose. But life does not end once we find purpose. We must begin to move toward our vision, to see it come together in reality. But what do we need to manifest it?

21

MANIFESTING WITH PURPOSE

Every worthwhile accomplishment, big or little, has its stages
of drudgery and triumph: a beginning, a struggle, and a victory.
~ *Mahatma Gandhi*

The first time we commit to manifesting our own vision is argu-ably the first time we're really living our own life. It can also be a moment of great conflict, both within ourselves and with the external world. Choosing to pursue our own vision may mean at the same time rejecting the expectations of others whose approval we may want. For some this can mean paying a heavy price, while for others these beginning steps may be much lighter. But in every case, the commitment to pursuing a vision requires that we begin to confront our differences with the reality of the external world.

Even if we believe the universe is ultimately helping us to manifest our visions, this does not mean the external world makes the path easy. Part of this is, ironically, because of us. We don't fundamentally choose visions based on how easy they are to achieve, but because they are a way for us to express our true selves. If we free ourselves from the demands of the external world when we create our visions, we may find the universe has not built most, or perhaps any, of what we see in our minds. It may even have placed something entirely different in front of us, and never bothered to ask us at all if we wanted it. None of this should come as a surprise. Life is not structured to give us the visions we choose on command simply because we desire them. If it was, the only challenge we would have in life would be to test the limits of our imagination when creating visions. We wouldn't need the will or determination to accomplish anything, only the ability to conjure it in our minds. But manifesting our visions in the reality of the external world is an important challenge we face, equal to the challenge of finding purpose. It requires us to remain connected to our true selves, to remain firmly grounded as we move forward.

The Status Quo and Our Vision

Depending on the vision we choose, the external world will respond based upon its own interests. If our vision easily fits within the external world's status quo, it will offer less resistance. These types of visions do not seek to fundamentally transform the power structure, conventional values, or other aspects of the social order in our society. By contrast, if our vision is a radical departure from the current structure of the external world, we should expect considerably more resistance. Visions that seek social change through modifying collective human behavior are some of the clearest examples of this because they need to alter the status quo substantially in order to succeed. The further our visions are from the external world's status quo, the more resistance we may face.

Facing greater resistance, or very little resistance, from the status quo does not necessarily mean one should change their vision. In each case, the most important consideration is that it really is your vision, and fits the real picture of you. It makes all the difference in the world if you are the one who really chose it, or if it was the external world that chose it for you. When some of my students successfully crafted their own visions and shared them with me, they would complain about the gap they saw with the external world. Two students in particular who came to my office embodied the reasons for their dissatisfaction.

Sarah was sitting in my office, wearing a sweatshirt with our school's name and black jeans that matched her black hair tied in a low ponytail. She began to tell me her vision was to do something that was in a prepackaged box already in front of her, which made her wonder why she was not creative or unique enough to have come up with anything more revolutionary. She had grown up being told by everyone around her she was to become a doctor, following in the footsteps of many others in her family tree. Although she initially rejected the idea, she came to realize after considerable self-reflection that being a doctor was also what *she* wanted.

When Jackie stopped by my office, she was wearing a black business suit with a white dress shirt and heels, the expected dress code for several school-wide events during the year. She began to tell me she was worried about how wide the gap was between her vision and reality, and wondered whether she had gone too far away from what the world expected from her. The daughter of two working-class, immigrant parents, she had just been admitted to one of the best law schools in the country, which had made her family immensely proud. There was just one problem: she had no desire to become a lawyer. She wanted to start her own health and wellness business, but had no idea where to begin.

Both students wondered "Why me?" but there is a clear answer to this question. We need *both* for our society to have any chance of a better future. We need those who find purpose in serving our world in its current form, otherwise we risk losing the progress we've already made. Our society isn't perfect, but it took us a lot of time and effort to get this far. We also need those whose visions are more radical. The reason our society has advanced at all is because there have always been those among us who had the courage and perseverance to change the world they were born into. There must always be those who have visions that are dramatically different from what we see today, because our society cannot change for the better without them.

Navigating with an Incomplete Map

Beyond addressing our differences with the external world, the process of manifesting visions also brings another challenge. While our initial starting point and desired end result may be clear, the exact path in between the two is often much less certain. And the further away our vision is from the status quo, the less clear the steps we need to take might be in the beginning. This may seem like an odd situation, like being handed a map where the entire area between your current location and your intended destination is blank, or at least very blurry. But this is part of the design of life—no one ever really knows exactly how they will get to their intended destination in the beginning. At best, we only have an idea, an initial plan. The more uncertain the road to achieving our vision is, the more we need to expect to adapt along the way. We may need to change course, take detours, be more tolerant of wrong turns, and remain even more conscious along the way, much like driving down an unfamiliar road in the darkness, with only a light far off in the distance to guide us. Needing to change our initial plan should never be confused with failure, because knowing the exact path beforehand with certainty cannot reasonably be expected when it's not part of life's fundamental design. To accurately evaluate our progress toward our intended destination, we need to assess how well we've adapted to the unexpected instead of measuring how far we've deviated from our initial plan. Manifesting visions is usually much more a result of successful adaptation as opposed to brilliant foresight in planning.

If you think you might struggle with not having a clear path at the outset to achieve your vision, you're not alone. My students struggled with this as well, and it's completely understandable. The process of manifesting visions is profoundly disconnected from what much of our education system teaches us about how the world works. It's much harder to evaluate students on how well they do in adapting to achieve something compared to following a predefined structure to solve well-understood problems. So, we prefer to teach the latter, because everybody in the system wins in the short term. Evaluation of student performance is clear and defensible, and students can even be ranked. Students like it because they have the comfort of a structure, a predictable code they can learn with enough repetition that gets them a better grade. But this isn't how life actually works, at least not if one is interested in manifesting their own vision. Even our best students are left unprepared to navigate the uncertainty that often comes with a path to real purpose, although they usually don't realize this until much later.

Most employers do no better than our schools, mainly because so much of the early phase of many careers is also highly structured. Usually, very little creative freedom exists in entry level jobs, with most work at the bottom of an organizational hierarchy being more routine than novel and groundbreaking. This remains true for a very long time in many career paths, if not for one's entire career. Organizations do face the challenge of navigating an uncertain world, but the responsibility of these challenges is reserved almost entirely for the management of the bureaucracy, who are typically much later in their careers. Places of employment can be great environments to gain a variety of valuable skills, but learning how to navigate an uncertain path to realizing one's vision is usually not one of them.

As we navigate the reality of the external world and continue to adapt, the achievement of our vision may start to become visible off in the distance, even if it's still far away. As we get closer, we may discover it doesn't look quite like we had pictured it in our mind at the outset. The setting may be a little different, the people around us may not be the people we had imagined, or other features may unexpectedly appear or be missing. This is to be expected, because what we saw in our vision is not meant to be a perfectly precise picture, only an approximation. And because it's not a perfect picture, manifesting does not necessarily mean one gets exactly what they had in their mind. However, this does not imply failure in any way. Achievement of a vision is not about how closely the reality that emerges matches with what we had imagined, but whether what appears is a satisfying and meaningful expression of our true selves; if it is, then we have successfully manifested our vision.

Another possibility that may occur is, we may discover our vision is no longer the right one for us to pursue, even if it may have seemed right for us at the outset. The process of manifesting isn't only about testing our persistence and determination to make our vision a reality; it also involves learning about ourselves through action, which is needed to complement the practice of conscious self-reflection. Working to manifest a vision is the most valuable type of experience we can have in learning more about ourselves, regardless of whether the vision itself is actually achieved. While one could argue that deciding to no longer pursue a vision is a sign of failure and wasted effort, this is a false interpretation. There is often no real substitute for the experience because no other way exists to gain the knowledge acquired. This can be an unavoidable and necessary part of one's evolution to purpose, as painful as it might feel.

Even after we understand all this, plenty of room for self-doubt remains during the process of manifesting our visions. This is part of the challenge life gives us, perhaps also by design. Visions are not guaranteed to manifest, and we face an unknown number of challenges ahead of us. Along the way, there are two moments where our self-doubt will be greatest:

- The first is at the very beginning, because we are taking the first steps on our own path.
- The second is when we face a challenge that seems insurmountable.

When the challenge appears, the critical voice in our mind

will tell us this surely is a sign we cannot go any further. If this aligns with our beliefs about how life works, then we'll be even more inclined to quit. Quitting may be the correct answer, but in order for it to be the right decision it cannot come from either the critical voice in our mind or our beliefs. Instead, it has to come from a different, less-biased point of view. When facing seemingly impossible challenges, fear and panic need to be turned off, and our mind must be stopped from imagining the worst-case scenario playing out as if it's already occurring. This usually requires taking a step back and clearing our minds until we can see things more objectively. And when we still can't find a solution to the challenge, there is one more thing we need to do: we need to call a member of our support group.

22

BUILDING YOUR
SUPPORT GROUP

Call it a clan, call it a network, call it a tribe, call it a family.
Whatever you call it, whoever you are, you need one.
~ Jane Howard

When we celebrate individuals who have achieved their visions, the way we do it gives the impression they accomplished their vision alone. If we honor them with an award or other form of recognition, we generally acknowledge only them and no one else. We may give generous praise for their efforts, but have little interest in hearing about who may have helped them and what they did. The idea that individuals can accomplish visions alone through their extraordinary abilities or remarkable determination is one we find eternally appealing, so much so, we are biased to tell the stories this way. If an individual also faces seemingly impossible odds of success, we relish the story even more. And while there are those among us who have achieved remarkable things entirely on their own, this is neither the most common path to a successful outcome nor the healthiest one. Rather than being lonely heroes in a struggle against the external world, we are much better off having others who support us on the path to realizing our vision, who we can call on in our times of need.

The Lonely Road Isn't the Best One

Seeking the support of others is not a sign of personal weakness, but an important part of how visions can be achieved. Significant accomplishments are often the product of a team effort, even if we are the ones driving. But pursuing our own vision can be challenging in part because doing so may mean choosing to be alone in the beginning, without the support we would ideally want. We may have no guides or others to help us, which may have been provided if we had instead done what the external world expected of us. In some cases, pursuing our vision means not only starting alone, but also facing active opposition from others. All of this can be understandably intimidating. Without greater understanding, this can convince us to stay within our current groups and do what's asked of us, even if doing so prevents us from pursuing our own vision. It may also seem reasonable to believe choosing to pursue our visions means we must be willing to walk the entire path without the support of others. This is almost never true, although believing it can become self-fulfilling. The evolution to purpose does not have to mean a commitment to being alone. The better approach is to find another way, a way to work toward our vision with others on our side as we move forward.

A pattern I saw repeatedly with my students was their capacity to achieve the visions they chose was not entirely a product of their own personal character. They often had others they could depend on and trust to give them both the wisdom and emotional fuel they needed to move forward. This was especially true during moments of what seemed like utter catastrophe, in seemingly hopeless situations where events could not be controlled and there appeared to be no solution. In these circumstances, having someone to talk to who was not clouded by the intense emotions these events created proved invaluable, either to provide helpful advice or to offer emotional support. Having these supportive people wasn't absolutely necessary to realizing their visions, but it did make achieving their visions less painful and difficult.

For many who are alone at the start of their path, this raises an obvious question: How does one build their support group? This can be more challenging than it sounds because most of us don't naturally choose who we associate with based on how supportive they would be in manifesting our visions. The friend we enjoy socializing with over drinks may not be reliable in helping us when we're panicking late at night, trying to deal with an urgent disaster. Our former boss, whose sage advice we would gladly have followed if we were in our old job, may have no helpful wisdom to offer us now as we work to manifest our vision. Unless we are lucky or have a list of friends so long that members of our support group can already be identified within our network, we have to work to consciously build it. It's a process of searching for the right people.

The Three Types of Members

When we're working to manifest our vision, we should ideally have three types of individuals in our support group:

- The first is **a mentor**, who has expertise that helps us achieve the vision we've chosen. They may not necessarily know exactly how to accomplish our vision, but they know what many of the steps are to get there. Often, these are people who have already accomplished something similar to what we're working toward.

- The second is **a coach**, who may not know the specific steps of how our particular vision can be achieved, but understands the state of mind required in order to walk the path to realizing one's vision. They know the universal structure of human achievement and can give us helpful feedback about how we're doing, including issues in our blind spots. Without someone to point them out to us, problems in our blind spots can pose a significant risk when working toward our vision because we cannot address what we cannot see.

- The third type of individual we should have in our support group is **a cheerleader**. Even if we have enough willpower to achieve our vision in isolation, it can be immensely helpful at times to get a burst of positive energy intended to help us feel better and more hopeful.

Of the three types of individuals one needs in their support group, the cheerleader is the most important. When we feel emotionally drained, our cheerleaders provide us with much-needed emotional fuel. If one has to choose between having the knowledge and resources needed to achieve a vision or enough emotional fuel, it's the latter that's far more important. Knowledge can always be gained and resources can always be gathered, but emotional fuel is the scarcest thing humans have. Not having enough of it is one of the biggest reasons why visions don't become reality. If we do have enough of it, almost all challenges and obstacles we face in life can eventually be overcome. If we want to achieve our visions, we need the emotional fuel to get there. We need enough fuel in our tank to drive along the highway, to reach our intended destination.

The "Dating" Process

Since building our support group is a search process, it's not entirely predictable where or when the right people can be found. At best, we can search based on educated guesses of where they might be and expect we may be wrong in many instances. Even if we do find people who in theory would be perfect, we may learn that in practice they aren't perfect for us. This is because building a support group is based not only on our choices, but the choices of everyone we connect with. And each of them has their own desires, values, and beliefs. If they decide to help us, it's usually because we're able to offer them something they value, or they have reason to like us enough to offer their support. Or, our vision may resonate strongly with them.

Finding the right people for our support group can be a frustrating process, the same way finding people in the world for any specific goal might be. One may find they encounter many of the wrong people, many "bad dates," before they find the right people for them. This is an expected part of the process, and is much more taxing if one does not enjoy meeting new people for its own sake. Many of my students struggled with this challenge, especially if they had too many bad dates in a row without meeting anyone who was a good fit. This is completely understandable, but not a good reason to give up. When my students persevered and eventually found great people who became part of their support group, they never felt they had worked too hard to find them, and that it hadn't been worthwhile. Finding the right people is always worth the effort.

Thankfully, having a well-functioning support group requires finding only a few individuals. If we find someone who can serve the role of more than one type of individual we need, then our group can be even smaller. While a few of my students had built large groups of people they felt they could rely on, most had support groups consisting of only a few trusted confidants. Very often they included family members, former coworkers, or close friends. Who they are and where we find them isn't important. What matters is whether they're the right people.

In addition to finding the right people, it also matters whether we have too many of the wrong people around us draining our emotional energy. For some of my students, choosing to pursue their own vision was met with disapproval, and at times hostility, from some of those around them. For these individuals, it turned out they did not accept or appreciate my students unconditionally, although this was not obvious to my students beforehand. Whether they were friends, family members, or others, they lacked a genuine understanding of who my students were. And they worked to drain my students of the emotional fuel needed to pursue their visions, often without realizing the harmful consequences of their behavior.

When trying to determine whether there are people in our life who drain our emotional fuel, a careful distinction must be made between those who give us genuinely helpful feedback that bruises our ego a little bit, and those who actively seek to drain us for their own interests. Those who give constructive feedback that helps us continuously improve to achieve our visions can be an invaluable part of our support group, and we need to keep our ego in check to make sure we can receive such feedback. Those who seek to drain us for their own purposes or satisfaction are not part of our support group, and must be managed. Whatever approach we use to manage them, enough distance must be maintained between them and our vision. Our emotional fuel is both precious and sacred, and must be treated as such.

After my students graduated and moved forward with their lives, I realized I was sometimes a member of their support group, and was able to observe what, if any, lasting impact the conversations in my office may have had.

Elizabeth was one student I had who experienced an especially dramatic and transformative shift in her consciousness before graduating. Breaking down in tears during her first visit to my office, she shared her struggles with, as she put it, "the expectations of our school." She hid it well, but she resented what she saw as the constant pressure to conform to our school's particular values and culture, and she especially disliked the choices of employers who came to campus, all of whom she seemed allergic to. "It's like being trapped in a restaurant where you don't want anything on the menu," she said. Although it wasn't planned, her initial visits to my office helped her gain clarity about herself and what she wanted; the later visits were little more than me reminding her it really was ok to do what she wanted, and watching her confidence grow. A reluctant contestant in our school's recruiting process, she decided to turn down a lucrative job offer in finance to pursue her own vision. Years later, she reached out and we spoke on the phone. She had never regretted turning down the job offer years ago, and concluded she surely would have been miserable if she had accepted it. She had creative urges that needed to be expressed, and wanted to be part of something that changed the status quo for the better. Ironically, upon graduation she joined a startup whose goal was to compete with the very same employer that had offered her a job. There had been some exhilarating and great moments in the subsequent years, and she felt successful. But, she admitted, there were also days where she wondered why she wasn't happier. "Isn't purpose supposed to make you happy?" she asked. She had, it seemed to her, done everything right. She had understood her true self as best as anyone could, and had the courage to pursue her vision. And it really was *her* vision. So, why wasn't she happier?

23

PURPOSE WILL MAKE YOU HAPPIER, BUT NOT EVERY DAY WILL BE A HAPPY ONE

For a long time it seemed to me that life was about to begin
—real life. But there was always some obstacle in the way,
something to be gotten through first, some unfinished business,
time still to be served, a debt to be paid. At last it dawned
on me that these obstacles were my life.
~ Alfred D'Souza

If one uses many of the most popular Hollywood movies as a guide for what life is like, they might conclude the beginning of doing anything worthwhile requires one to deal with a series of difficult challenges. Once these challenges have been overcome, one achieves a happy ending that lasts forever, or at least a very long time. The external threats one has to face dissolve with the satisfying conclusion of victory. If any internal conflicts exist, which often include self-doubt, indisputable success makes them vanish into the past. Relationships that may have been damaged by conflict are restored by reaching an almost magical degree of mutual understanding and respect, often with very little dialogue. At the end of the movie, the protagonists we sympathize with, who are clearly good people we like, feel great about a job well done. And when we see them in this moment, we share the same feeling. All is right in the world again.

Of course, we all know life doesn't work this way. The happy endings of Hollywood movies are difficult to find in real life. Old external threats and internal conflicts can return, and new ones can emerge. Relationships may never reach a point of mutual understanding and respect, regardless of how much dialogue takes place. We all know these things, but we often wish life worked like these movies, to the point where we may feel disappointed when we discover it doesn't. The actors and actresses in the movies we see can be pretty convincing. But the reality is that life is much less perfect or simple. While working to manifest our visions can make us happier, it's not the happiness of a Hollywood ending, even when we achieve what we set out to do. If we do happen to experience it, the moment is only fleeting. What we see in Hollywood movies is not what a better life actually looks like. But what is it supposed to look like, then?

Life Is Challenges More Than Triumphs

A core part of the experience of life is how we deal with challenges. We can choose to run away from them, face them head on, or address them in another way, but we must always deal with them somehow. Sometimes we choose which challenges we face, and in other cases the challenges simply appear in front of us, against our own wishes. If one looks closely at how we spend our time over our entire working lives, the vast majority of our life is spent working to overcome the challenges we face, not celebrating our victories. This is not because we're not good enough or fast enough, or lacking in some other way. It's how life is designed. No matter how hard we try, the incredible feeling we get from being victorious inevitably fades far quicker than we'd like, and then it's over. When measured by the amount of time spent in different emotional states, most of the quality of our lives is determined not by how we feel the moment we achieve our visions, but when we're dealing with challenges.

At first glance, if one has to choose between dealing with the challenges of pursuing their own vision or consciously avoiding challenges altogether, the latter might seem more appealing. Challenges can be daunting, and dealing with them can lead to painful experiences. The most straightforward way one might avoid challenges is to live without intention and take a passive approach to life. From this perspective, being active with intention is the surest way to run into challenges, so one can choose instead to have no intention. This is a form of withdrawal from life itself, and when it does happen it initially resembles one simply taking a break from whatever path they've been pursuing. However, unlike breaks that refresh us for our next challenge, one gradually surrenders into a more permanent state of inactivity. Some of my older students were in this state when they visited my office, which taught me that just because one appeared to be alive did not mean they were actually living.

As one example, Jason was a student of mine who had descended deep into this catatonic state by the time he visited my office. The energy in the room dropped instantly the moment he stepped into my office, and the tired strands of gray hair remaining on his head confounded his true age. When he shared his story, I learned he had once been passionate about achieving lofty goals with his work but experienced a series of painful setbacks, including an entrepreneurial venture with childhood friends that ended in ruin after their betrayal. He had accepted an unfulfilling marketing job with a large pharmaceutical company in part because it offered a high degree of job security, but struggled to find the motivation to do even the bare minimum of what was expected. His outlook struck me as that of someone who was waiting to die, with no real goals or aspirations left. He did what was necessary to survive and fulfill what was expected of him, but had forgotten the story of his life. There was no vision. But rather than being happier with his life because of his choices, he had grown progressively more miserable and lost, as the passive approach he took yielded its predictable outcome.

Although living without intention is a path to unhappiness, the desire to avoid emotional pain is not a compelling enough reason on its own for one to pursue their own vision, because the path to achieving one's vision often also includes painful experiences. However, while the negative emotions from both may feel similarly unpleasant, the potential value each has for our lives is dramatically different. Given that life is structured to only reward those who take an active approach to living, one learns little from the negative emotions that arise from taking a passive approach other than how painful it can be. As I've mentioned before, these negative emotions are often interpreted as evidence one is too small or powerless to battle an infinitely stronger universe. But this is a misunderstanding of the true signal from these emotions.

The message is meant to be much simpler, and does not need to be overanalyzed: We are designed to operate with intention, and living without it for too long violates something inside us.

By contrast, negative emotions we feel when pursuing our vision can tell us something much more valuable. On the path to achieving our vision, negative emotions usually arise when difficult or unforeseen challenges emerge. They may point out areas within ourselves we need to improve, provide information about circumstances in the external world that signal an adaptation is needed, or, in some cases, tell us our vision is not the right one for us. These emotions may not feel pleasant, but they give us information that's far more useful to move forward in our lives than if we lived without intention. The negative emotions we feel during these experiences offer insight into ourselves and the world around us, helping us to grow into who we were meant to be. When observing the struggles many of my students had, I wondered if there was perhaps another, less painful way they could gain the same insight. If there was, I could tell others, and make their paths easier. At the very least, I wondered whether some of my students who had gone through particularly painful experiences could see an easier way they might have learned the same lessons. To find out, I dared to ask a few whose paths had been especially difficult. Surprisingly, none of them were able to honestly imagine an easier path for themselves, given who they were and what they knew at the time. Some things, one cannot really expect to learn in any other way.

If the benefit of pursuing our own vision is not to live every day with the happiness of a Hollywood ending, and following our own path also includes painful experiences just as living without intention does, how are we better off? Gaining insight is valuable, but is that all we gain? At the beginning of this book, I said the vast majority of us spend more of our waking lives working than doing anything else, which means it matters tremendously how we feel at work, especially over a long period of time. And while there can be many factors that determine how one feels at work, I observed from my students two factors that were especially important: the people one worked with, and why they did the work.

Lucky with People, Deliberate with Purpose

For my students who were working in full-time jobs, one pattern I noticed that surprised me was how much of their happiness at work was simply a product of being lucky enough to be around people who they worked well with. I say lucky because it really was luck—they usually had little or no control over who they worked with, and things just happened to work well for a period of time. However, when the people around them were replaced with others they didn't work well with, they began to enjoy their job much less, and some seriously considered quitting altogether. In many cases, it was clear the only real reason they enjoyed their jobs until that point was the people they worked with, and not the actual work itself. The people made the work enjoyable, but often the work did not make the people even tolerable. Whether they realized it or not, my students got much of their emotional fuel from the people around them.

If we work long enough, we will inevitably run into people who affect us emotionally both positively and negatively. In a perfect world with a Hollywood ending, we would reach a point of mutual respect and understanding with those who cause us to feel negative emotions or simply remove them entirely, and our problems would be solved. But in reality, we usually have little ability to do this. Even if we leave our employer, we're still gambling that a new environment will be a much better place, which is always uncertain. As important as people are to how we feel at work, we usually have little control over who we have to deal with. What we have much more control over is the work we choose to do.

When we deal with challenges that emerge in life, we may understandably have painful experiences that drain us emotionally. As I've mentioned before, the ultimate difference between whether we achieve our visions or not is often the amount of emotional fuel we have to continue. To avoid running out of fuel and being stuck, the part of our mind that asks us "Why are you doing this?" needs to be satisfied with the answer we give. This is meant to help us, and prevent us from choosing to experience negative emotions without good reason. The better the answer we give, the more fuel we will have to power us in moving forward. And the more fuel we have at any given moment, the happier we are. The same way we need enough food to nourish us for our physical health, we need enough emotional fuel for us to experience a high quality of life. If we don't eat enough, we become physically weaker. If we don't have a good-enough reason for why we are dealing with the painful experiences that come with life's challenges, we become emotionally weaker. And being emotionally weaker limits how good we feel, because we lose the strength needed to achieve what we can visualize in our minds.

Choosing work that gives us a sense of purpose is necessary to experience the highest quality of life: an empowered state of being. When we create and pursue visions that reflect who we really are, we assemble the greatest emotional strength we have. This strength creates a version of us that operates at our highest potential, increasing many of the elements we need to be happier. We have a stronger foundation to be more confident, and more resilient. Much like how someone who is much stronger physically may be easily spotted by others, those around us may also notice we are emotionally much stronger than most, and look to us for support, inspiration, and even leadership. This comes from being the best version of ourselves, manifesting our own vision and telling everyone what we are here to do, in the clearest terms.

24

THE DEATHBED TEST

Human stories are practically always about one thing,
really, aren't they? Death.
~ J.R.R. Tolkien

If humans truly have the gift of free will, then we all have the power to choose what to do with the lives we've been given. But there are some conditions. We cannot control many things we encounter in the external world. We know the time we have been given is finite, but we don't know exactly how long we have. And whatever we choose to do, we cannot know with certainty what will actually happen. At the beginning of our lives most of us spend little time thinking about this, and the only reality we know is dominated by the highly structured and predictable environment of our education system. But once we complete our formal education, we enter the real world as adults. From that moment on almost anything can happen, depending on what we decide to do with our lives. Having a strong sense of purpose will give us a happier, better quality of life. Is there a way to confirm that we're making the right decisions?

If we knew when we would die, we might think of life as a block of time we've been given to accomplish the things we want to get done. Maybe we'd like to build something that will outlive our time on Earth. Maybe we'd like to find a life partner, and maybe even have children. If we knew the day our life would end, we would make sure to do everything we could to get these things done. We would be more aware of whether we were spending too much time doing things we didn't really care about, and if we were neglecting the things we really wanted to do. But we don't actually know when our last day will be. And death is an uncomfortable reality off in the distance, one we're usually able to ignore on any given day. We can easily lose track of time, and begin to believe we will always have plenty of time to do what we want later. This phenomenon is so common that one has to wonder, if humans lived forever, whether many of us would ever end up doing what we really want to do.

In modern society, our approach to the reality of death is mostly one of avoidance. We grudgingly accept there will be a day we will no longer be here, but generally give it little to no thought unless we're forced to. As I've mentioned earlier in the book, for some people I knew it took the death of a loved one for them to become more conscious. For some, this fits their belief about how one lives fully, by operating as if they will live forever until they cannot. In a society where death is a reality to be kept out of one's mind, the people who tend to pay more attention to it are those who may be considering ending their own life. But the reality of death was never meant to be handled in this way, and many of our ancestors had much healthier ways of addressing it within their cultures. Death is a fundamental part of life, and is perhaps the most important aspect of life all human beings have in common, as different as we may think we are from each other.

Reflecting on Our Death

Reflecting on the reality of our death may not be exciting or pleasurable, but it serves as a powerful tool for increasing our consciousness. It's something we know is coming for certain, and it's the reason why life is so valuable. Reflecting on it is a way to make sure we have not fallen asleep while leaving the autopilot button on. Often, even a small increase in awareness can lead to a realization of how much our immediate concerns are not that important in the grander scheme of life. If we continue to reflect, we may also begin to see just how much our own personal interests have been neglected. In that moment, a voice in our minds will begin to provide a long list of reasons justifying the neglect, arguing that there was no other way. Having heard this voice frequently emerge from the students who visited my office, I observed that this was almost never the full and true story, although there were enough grains of truth that one might be fooled to think it was. If we reflect further, these justifications become less convincing, and we recognize the time we have left is much more precious than we thought. Contemplating the reality of one's death is not a morbid fascination with dying or desiring to end one's life; it is the exact opposite. If we are more conscious of the reality of our lives being finite, then we appreciate just how valuable our lives really are, and we're better able to focus on what really matters to us.

Some of the most difficult conversations I had in my office were with some of my older students who seemed to have taken every wrong turn imaginable to end up where they were. The wrong turns were not wrong by the standards of the external world, but at each point their emotions had tried to signal their direction was wrong, only to be repeatedly ignored. Ironically, some of them had already achieved enough success by society's standards that they had been invited to speak in front of younger audiences as positive role models. But rather than feeling energized by the recognition and validation, they felt miserable and fake. They weren't sitting in my office because they were unsure of whether they had made the right decisions—their emotions already clearly answered that for them. They had come because they realized there was only a finite amount of time left in their lives, and didn't want to spend the rest of their lives feeling the same way.

What made these conversations difficult wasn't anything about their challenges or their personalities. It was hearing the stories of how they spent so much of their lives denying who they were, causing a terrible amount of self-inflicted pain. Many of them relied upon the pleasures money could buy—expensive luxury clothes, fine dining, travel to exotic destinations—to compensate for the lack of joy and satisfaction with their work, which ultimately failed to be enough. And it was greater awareness of the limited time they had left that pushed them to consider making significant changes in their lives.

If a healthy part of consciously living life is to maintain awareness of its temporary nature, how exactly are we supposed to do it? One simple and practical way of doing this is the deathbed test. Imagine you are on your deathbed, in your final days of life, looking back on yourself right now at the present moment. How does your future self feel about what you are doing right now?

Is it happy and satisfied with what you're doing? If it's not, why does it feel the way it does? If you try this and are struggling, this is either because you don't know your true self well enough yet, the reality of death is too distant from your life right now, or both. Understanding ourselves better comes with the practice of self-reflection, and a deeper understanding of the finite nature of life is inevitable if one is simply patient. Until then, the test is something that will still work to a degree, and will become more powerful and useful over time as you practice it.

The deathbed test is effective because it does multiple things simultaneously that are needed to give us the right perspective.

- First, it removes what everyone else expects and wants from us, because when we're on our deathbed we don't care as much anymore about the demands of the external world. Many of us struggle to even dream of a life without such demands, to the point where it only becomes possible when we imagine we are about to die.
- Second, it increases our consciousness of the reality of death without having to guess when our life may end. We don't know when our last days will be, but we can always imagine that moment and look back on the present.
- And finally, it allows us to evaluate any decisions we currently have to make from a longer-term perspective, which aligns more closely with how pivotal life decisions should usually be considered.

Living life without being conscious is often too focused on dealing with the immediate problems one faces at any given moment, which can consume an entire lifetime without going in any particular direction or accomplishing anything personally meaningful. But if we become more aware of the finite nature of our lives, we are unlikely to continue living this way.

Clarity from Our Deathbed

While we can't know with certainty if the choices we make will produce the outcomes we desire, we can know in advance if they are what we want to do. In this sense, we know if what we are about to do is the right decision for us. The deathbed test helps us clarify, when the time we have is precious and limited, what is most important to us. One might argue this is very hard to evaluate if there are too many things that are important to us, but this is rarely what happens in practice. Most of us have only a few things we really value in our lives, especially if we apply the deathbed test. *The problem we usually have is not that we have too many important things to do, but that we are doing too many things that aren't actually that important to us.*

In theory, one could argue that making the right decision really depends not on how we feel before we see the result, but on the outcome that actually occurs. From this perspective, the deathbed test has little value because it doesn't evaluate the outcome, and instead should be replaced with a judgment of the most likely outcome in the future. Such an approach is usually an inevitable weighing of probabilities, costs, and benefits, with our rational mind taking the lead to make our decision. For pivotal life decisions, this argument is not only problematic, but usually destined to fail by design if we want to be happy. As I've mentioned before, our rational mind does a poor job of assessing our emotions, especially with how happy future outcomes will make us feel. It's also poorly suited for taking the lead in making pivotal life decisions because there just isn't enough data for our rational mind to estimate with confidence what will happen next. Life just isn't that predictable, and it never has been.

If we instead follow the deathbed test for our pivotal life decisions, we know we will choose to do whatever is truly important to us. And there are some basic truths that come with taking this road over the many others we can follow in life. Doing what we think is most important is going to give us a much stronger sense of purpose than doing what we think is less important. This provides a much more satisfying answer for why we're doing what we're doing, which helps us achieve our visions. And, ironically, it will matter much less how much the external world will reward us for what we do, because we will be less dependent on the external world to feel positive emotions. Once we become more conscious of life as a finite block of time we have to work with, we will realize the responsibility we have to ourselves not to waste it or live with regret, and to maintain our focus on doing what matters.

25

LIFE ON THE PATH OF PURPOSE

Nothing will work unless you do.
~ Maya Angelou

The last few centuries have demonstrated dramatic progress in humanity's evolution. The technologies we have today are many times faster, smarter, and more capable than what our ancestors used, and it seems inevitable that future generations will look back at us amazed by our primitive tools. Beyond our technological progress, we have also made significant improvements in our quality of life. We can expect to live much longer and physically healthier lives than our ancestors, and we know considerably more than they did about almost every subject. Our expanded knowledge has multiplied the choices we have to accomplish what we want, substantially increasing our ability to manifest what we create in our minds. We also have more freedom to do what we want in life than our ancestors could ever have imagined. All of this provides good reason to be optimistic about the future. But none of this is enough to ensure our lives, or those of future generations, will actually be any happier.

Trying to predict the future of our society is often the work of science fiction writers, who present a version of how life may look in the distant future in order to tell their stories. Many of these future worlds are much more technologically advanced, but ultimately dystopian. Despite being very successful at building much better machines, humanity fails to build a better society where people are happier. Given our society's current design, it's not hard to see how one could imagine a future that reflects such lopsided progress. But for our own lives, it doesn't have to be this way. Even if the external world has little interest in seeing us explore or express our true selves, we can choose to take our own path. We can choose the path of purpose, and evolve beyond the machinery that shapes us.

Finding our purpose requires us to have a sufficient level of consciousness, which begins with a greater awareness of who we truly are. This is something that cannot be expected to happen naturally, because having it is not necessary for us to either survive or succeed by the standards of our society. It may come easily to a lucky few, but most often happens through a deliberate practice of self-reflection we must maintain regularly. We have to make the space and time to know ourselves better. Deliberate effort is needed because we are surrounded by powerful and addictive forces that can easily distract us, all of which work to keep us unconscious. Without being more aware of who we are, we won't know what to do if our emotions tell us we're headed in the wrong direction. We need to begin to solve the puzzle of who we are first.

As we look within ourselves, we also look out into the external world to understand both its demands and opportunities. Its demands will have little interest in us as individuals beyond a few things it judges to be useful, and will work to place us in a predefined box as quickly as possible. Our education system will measure our value and grade us for employers, who will have boxes waiting for each of us. One box will lead to another box, and then another. It's the machinery of how our society works, to make the best use of us it knows how. But it doesn't really know us. This is why the opportunities are so important. The external world also offers building blocks we can use to manifest visions we create. Instead of following what the machinery tells us to do, we can have a life that's uniquely ours.

Being a professor gave me a unique perspective that allowed me to see patterns in the lives of my students, both younger and older. These patterns, I realized, represent a much bigger picture of all of us and how we live. Once these patterns came together, my own awareness changed, and I began to see more clearly why so much of the world was unhappy every day at work. I also started to see what the true cost of this phenomenon looked like. Some had resigned from life, drained of the emotional fuel they had when they were younger. Others hadn't withdrawn, but quietly endured astonishing amounts of emotional pain which they had somehow learned to live with, diminishing their quality of life. Until I got to know many of my students, I had been unaware of the extent and prevalence of these problems because almost everyone who suffers does so in silence, as if they had been told that how they felt was something no one cared to hear. The patterns I observed were so consistent and so common that I realized these issues could not reflect something unusual about a few isolated individuals. They were the consequence of the way we have designed our society, including our education system and employers. Perhaps we are closer to the dystopian society of the future than we think. But if we know this, we really can do something about it. And it is never too late.

There are good reasons to choose the path of purpose, but it is often not the easiest path one can take, especially in the short run. However, a fundamental principle of life seems to be that consistently following what is easiest and least painful is unlikely to ever lead to genuine happiness. If it did, many more people would be happier with the work they have chosen to do. For whatever reason, life seems intended not to be easy, but necessarily challenging. A happier life is not defined then by having fewer or easier challenges, but by our emotional state when we are dealing with the inevitable challenges life brings us. And we have a choice with at least some of the challenges we face. We can choose those challenges that give us a sense of purpose. And because our conscious decision is always required, living a life of purpose isn't something that just happens to us; it's the product of our intention.

At the outset, one who chooses to follow the demands of the external world and one who follows their own vision may appear to be doing the same thing, but over a long-enough time frame an enormous difference exists in their quality of life. I know because I've seen it repeatedly, over and over again in my students. Even if they both make it to the same finish line and are equally celebrated by the external world, they will not experience it in the same way. One will feel much less satisfaction, and the triumph of victory will be more hollow. The praise from others will be appreciated, but will do little to fill the emptiness inside them. By contrast, the other will have a much greater sense of satisfaction when getting to the finish line. Recognition by others will also be appreciated, and provide the additional gratification that comes with seeing that the external world has acknowledged the legitimacy of their vision. They will feel like a great success. And the only successful people in this world are the ones who feel successful. There is no other meaningful definition.

The freedom to choose is the gift we've been given, but how wisely we use it depends entirely on us. Whatever we choose to do, it will ultimately become self-fulfilling. One who squanders the gift they've been given has a lot in common with the one who never had it to begin with, and one who uses it well will evolve to look and think differently. Many examples exist of both types of individuals in the world, each of whom believe they have discovered an important truth in life. Many of my students, never having been told they had true freedom of choice, simply followed what was placed in front of them, which was often what was expected of them by the external world. But the world offers many more possibilities than what is right in front of us, if one becomes more conscious and notices the other paths. Many of those who choose to pursue their visions offer proof of this all the time. If Ryan Reynolds, Colonel Sanders, Oprah Winfrey, Kiran Mazumdar-Shaw, Robin Li, and Albert Einstein all started out accepting what the external world gave them, we never would have seen what they could do. What we decide to do has profound implications for our future happiness, although we rarely comprehend this fully when we make our choice. Of the different paths we can take, the path of purpose is the only one where we come into alignment with our true selves. Only then can we live our own lives, and not the lives of other people. This is the life we were always meant to have, by design.

THE KEYS TO PURPOSE

This book is about a different life path you can choose to take, if you become conscious enough. But as with all consciously chosen paths, we can easily fall back into the life we had before because we forget what we've learned. Our environments often don't encourage our new way of life at the outset, so we have to work to continue to see clearly in the beginning until the energy in our environment changes to support us. The following are some key ideas to help you maintain a clear view as you move forward on your new path.

1. Our society is not designed to help us find purpose. Much of our world looks the way it does because it is the outcome of our society's design. This includes the many people who work without a strong sense of purpose. Our society is designed to address some of our needs, such as our need for food and shelter, but does little to help us meet our need for purpose. If we simply do what society places in front of us without being more conscious, we will probably never come to know our true purpose.

2. We can evolve beyond our society's design. In fact, one could argue we were always supposed to. We can better understand our true self and how the external world works, and then make choices that are truly our own. This is the only way to find lasting happiness at work—and more generally in our lives—because we will always be too complicated and unique for society's design to ever lead us there. Many of our ancestors never had the choice to become anything more than what they were born into, despite their own unique potential and complex needs. But we are not living in the same world as they did. The opportunity to evolve has never been bigger, better, or more exciting.

3. Purpose comes from knowing our true self, never from following the external world. Our true self is real, but we can easily fail to appreciate this if we can't clearly see ourselves. This state of not knowing makes us vulnerable to external influences and interests. If we don't know our true self, then a confident-sounding voice from the external world telling us who we are is easy to believe. The many competitions we enter and the behavior we see from those around us can shape our knowledge and sense of reality so strongly that we may have no real understanding of ourselves at all. But even in these extreme circumstances our true self will send us signals, usually in the form of unpleasant emotions that may feel confusing at first. These signals are trying to tell us something that has always been true, but is often forgotten: purpose comes from aligning our life with our true self, not from following the external world.

4. Having a vision is what creates certainty in an uncertain world. As I said at the beginning of this book, we really have no idea what's possible for us, and we also don't know what will actually happen in our life. That's part of life's design. But we can create an image of what we would like to see in our future—our vision. This doesn't eliminate the uncertainty of whether our vision becomes a reality, but it does eliminate the uncertainty about our focus and intention. By creating a vision, we know with certainty what we intend to do, even if the universe doesn't provide certainty about anything else. In an uncertain world, certainty is created by us.

5. Feeling fear is natural when both creating and manifesting visions; it is not a sign of weakness. If you're struggling to think of successful people who let fear dominate their pivotal life decisions, it's because being controlled by fear isn't how visions are created or manifested. This isn't to say risks should be ignored, but evaluating risk and being fearful are not the same thing. If you're feeling afraid, ask yourself whether your fear is clouding your decisions and judgment. Then ask what you would decide to do if you didn't feel afraid, and how you might instead manage the risks you see, to ensure physical survival. If your decision doesn't change at all or only a little, you are managing your fear effectively.

6. Achieving visions is less a matter of being good enough, and more a matter of finding enough emotional fuel. Every moment where one believes they cannot continue further to achieve their vision has one thing in common: they have run out of emotional fuel (remember, this is the energy that powers us to accomplish our goals). It's understandable to conclude our inability to continue is because we are not "good enough," but it's more accurate to say we haven't reached our goal yet and have simply lost the energy to continue. With few exceptions, emotional fuel is the defining factor that leads to achievement, or never making it to the finish line. Those who achieve simply have more emotional fuel, either because they chose a vision that provided them with more fuel to begin with, or because they were able to find more in moments where they ran out. The latter is especially important, because we almost never have enough at the outset to take us to the end. If you have an effective way to replenish your emotional fuel, you have found one of the most precious resources in life.

7. *Not knowing how you will achieve your vision is ok; not learning how is not.* Creating a vision sets a destination on the map of your life, but often does not immediately reveal the exact way to get there. This is also part of life's design, and not a reason for panic or feeling discouraged. The next step is always one of learning how to reach your vision, which can feel overwhelming, uncomfortable, and scary. These feelings are natural, especially because we were never taught how to manage risk in life. Remember, you are simply running experiments at the beginning which won't threaten your physical survival, trying to see what works. If something doesn't work, it doesn't say anything about you. Instead, it's time to use the knowledge gained to set up the next experiment. Once something does work, the way will suddenly become much clearer on the map, and you will know where to go.

8. *Seeing clearly requires a ritual practice of self-reflection.* Unless you have completely isolated yourself from the world, your environment will constantly seek to demand your attention in every way it can. Some of these demands will be important; most will not. All of them will distort your ability to see clearly to

at least some extent. A regular practice of self-reflection, including the many forms of meditation, corrects this distortion. Do you know what you would see if all the distractions and external voices around you were removed, and the voices in your head grew quiet? You cannot know what's there when your eyes are closed. That is, until you open them. Also, a practice of self-reflection is not a practice of self-criticism or repeated frustration. That's why monks will chant mantras or repeat simple exercises to reflect, not judgmental statements of themselves or others. One creates a clearer, deeper understanding of the nature of our situation, while the other makes us blind.

9.   *A life of purpose is more about how one feels most days when working, and less about what one will accomplish.* This book is really about how we feel during the time we spend dealing with challenges—most of the days of our lives—not the brief moments when we finally see the outcome of our work. It's about being able to say we had a good day at work because we know what we're doing is important, and that we're supposed to be doing it. That's what being happier at work really means—making sure most of our days are good ones, not just the few days we see the final outcomes.

10.   *Evolving to a life of purpose is actually the story of a hero's triumph.* Don't believe me? Maybe you never thought of yourself as a hero. In every hero's story, they must go out into an uncertain world and face challenges that test them, often to their limits of ability, courage, and belief. They face plenty of struggles, and the outcome is never certain. After the battles are completed, they are no longer the same as when they first ventured out. They are

stronger, wiser, and know the value of what they have done. They have also learned the important lessons they were meant to learn. Each of us has the chance to be a hero in our own life story. What would happen if we took that chance?

WHERE DO I GO FROM HERE?

Thank you for taking the time to read this book. Like any author who is passionate about their message, I've enjoyed having the chance to share my work with you. For many of you, this book is just the first step of an exciting—and perhaps scary—new path of independence from the machinery that shapes us. To follow the latest developments in the evolution of my work, you can visit:

www.evolutiontopurpose.com

ACKNOWLEDGMENTS

The journey that led to this book was helped by others who added their own enthusiasm and curiosity along the way. Few of my many research assistants over the years were spared at least one task investigating some aspect of happiness at work, but several were especially dedicated, either to the cause or to humoring their eccentric professor: Jessica Guo, Laura Tichelman, Jane Jiang, Kairi Vaikla, Brandon Kucera, Akshanta Ajay, Sydra Stoner, Ashley Hong, and Samantha Wu. A debt of gratitude is owed to Lynn Imai, Kapil Nair, and Davis Fattedad for providing feedback on an early draft of this book, and to Kate Haugan for her meticulous review of it just before its release. I also thank Lisa Bess Kramer at Cleveland Edits for her editing, and Lisa Hagan of Lisa Hagan Literary for introducing us.

ABOUT THE AUTHOR

Dr. Bryan Hong has taught as a professor at the New York University Leonard N. Stern School of Business, The Wharton School at the University of Pennsylvania, and Ivey Business School in Canada. He received his PhD from the University of California-Berkeley and currently teaches at the Henry W. Bloch School of Management at the University of Missouri-Kansas City. Prior to beginning his academic career, he previously worked in investment banking, corporate strategic planning, and business strategy consulting. His greatest personal productivity hack is being a digital nomad at least once a year. He lives with his wife in Kansas City.

ENDNOTES

1. Paul Dolan makes a good case for this in his discussion of happiness. (see Dolan, P. *Happiness by design: Change what you do, not how you think.* UK: Penguin, 2014.)

2. One related example is Olympic athletes who win the silver medal, who tend to be less happy than those who win the bronze medal. This is because silver medalists compare their outcome to possibly winning the gold, while bronze medalists generally compare to possibly not winning any medal. (see Medvec VH, Madey SF, Gilovich T. "When less is more: counterfactual thinking and satisfaction among Olympic medalists." *Journal of Personality and Social Psychology* 69, no. 4 (November 1995): 603-610.)

3. Norton, M. I., Mochon, D., Ariely, D. "The IKEA effect: When labor leads to love." *Journal of Consumer Psychology* 22, no. 3 (2012): 453-460; Inzlicht, M., Shenhav, A., Olivola, C. Y. "The effort paradox: Effort is both costly and valued." *Trends in Cognitive Sciences* 22, no. 4 (2018): 337-349.

4. Loewenstein, G. "Because it is there: The challenge of mountaineering... for utility theory." Kyklos 52, no. 3 (1999): 315-344; Simpson, D., Post, P. G., Young, G., Jensen, P. R. "'It's not about taking the easy road': The experiences of ultramarathon runners." The Sport Psychologist 28, no. 2 (June 2014): 176-185.

5. Dohle, S., Rall, S., Siegrist, M. "I cooked it myself: Preparing food increases liking and consumption." *Food Quality and Preference* 33 (2014): 14-16.

6. A few examples of people who have publicly acknowledged relying heavily on their intuition are Richard Branson, Steve Jobs, and Oprah Winfrey. (see Tabaka, M. "Iconic entrepreneurs use their intuition to succeed. What you need to know about following your gut." *Inc.*, September 30, 2019. https://www.inc.com/marla-tabaka/iconic-entrepreneurs-use-their-intuition-to-succeed-what-you-need-to-know-about-following-your-gut. html)

7. The rational mind I refer to here is similar to the rational mind described in Dialectical Behavioral Therapy. There are also a number of studies that show humans make systematic errors in predicting how future events will make them feel. (see Linehan, M.M. *Cognitive behavioral therapy of borderline personality disorder.* New York: Guilford Press, 1993; Wilson, T. D., Gilbert, D. T. "Affective forecasting." In *Advances in experimental social psychology*, edited by M. P. Zanna, 345-411. New York: Elsevier, 2003.)

8. Pak, E. "Walt Disney's Rocky Road to Success." Biography. June 17, 2020. https://www.biography.com/news/walt-disney-failures

9. Gabler, N. *Walt Disney: The Triumph of the American Imagination*. New York: Vintage, 2006.

10. Kuznets, S. *National Income 1929–1932. A report to the U.S. Senate, 73rd Congress, 2nd Session.* Washington, DC: US Government Printing Office, 1934.

11. Kesternich, I., Siflinger, B., Smith, J. P., Winter, J. K. "The effects of World War II on economic and health outcomes across Europe." *Review of Economics and Statistics* 96, no. 1 (2014): 103-118.

12. Costanza, R., Hart, M., Talberth, J., Posner, S. "Beyond GDP: The need for new measures of progress." Boston: Pardee Center for the Study of the Longer-Range Future, 2009.

13. Oxford Poverty & Human Development Initiative. "Bhutan's Gross National Happiness Index." Accessed December 20, 2021. https://ophi.org.uk/policy/gross-national-happiness-index/

14. Easton, P. *Sustaining Literacy in Africa: Developing a Literate Environment.* Paris: United Nations Educational, Scientific and Cultural Organization, 2014.

15. A wide range of institutions have historically been used to coerce individuals to engage in work that societies required. Although it may be hard to imagine today, for most of human history institutionalized coercive working relationships were extremely common throughout the world, with only a small percentage of workers having the level of freedom many of us take for granted. (see Eltis, D., Engerman, S. L., eds. *The Cambridge world history of slavery: Volume 3, AD 1420–AD 1804.* Cambridge: Cambridge University Press, 2011.)

16. Meyer, J. W., Ramirez, F. O., Soysal, Y. N. "World expansion of mass education, 1870-1980." *Sociology of education* 65, no. 2 (1992): 128-149; Goldin, C. "Human Capital." In *Handbook of Cliometrics*, edited by C. Diebolt and M. Haupert, 55-86. Heidelberg, Germany: Springer-Verlag, 2016.

17. Moatsos, M. "Global extreme poverty: Present and past since 1820." In *How Was Life? Volume II: New Perspectives on Well-being and Global Inequality since 1820.* Paris: OECD Publishing, 2021.

18. Improving incentives for teachers continues to be an ongoing area of research. (see Dee, T. S., Wyckoff, J. (2015). "Incentives, selection, and teacher performance: Evidence from IMPACT." *Journal of Policy Analysis and Management* 34, no. 2 (2015): 267-297; Fryer, R. G. "Teacher incentives and student achievement: Evidence from New York City public schools." *Journal of Labor Economics* 31, no. 2 (2013): 373-407.)

19. The most extreme version of this phenomenon is likely to be in business schools, and perhaps other professional schools.

20. Cappelli, P. *The New Deal at Work.* Boston: Harvard Business School Press, 1999; Bidwell, M. J. "What happened to long-term employment? The role of worker power and environmental turbulence in explaining declines in worker tenure." *Organization Science* 24, no. 4 (2013): 1061-

1082.

21. Kalleberg, A. L., Vallas, S. P. "Probing precarious work: Theory, research, and politics." *Research in the Sociology of Work* 31, no. 1 (2018): 1-30.

22. Numerous examples throughout history can be found in Eltis, D., Engerman, S. L., eds. *The Cambridge world history of slavery: Volume 1-4*. Cambridge: Cambridge University Press, 2011.

23. Kanigel, R. *The One Best Way: Frederick Winslow Taylor and the Enigma of Efficiency*. New York: Viking Books, 1997.

24. McGonigal, K. "Five Surprising Ways Exercise Changes Your Brain." *Greater Good Magazine*. January 6, 2020. https://greatergood.berkeley. edu/article/item/five_surprising_ways_exercise_changes_your_brain; Alter, A. *Irresistible: The rise of addictive technology and the business of keeping us hooked*. New York: Penguin, 2017; Cleveland Clinic "Why Retail 'Therapy' Makes You Feel Happier." January 21, 2021. https://health. clevelandclinic.org/retail-therapy-shopping-compulsion/; Aguinaga, D., Medrano, M., Vega-Quiroga, I., Gysling, K., Canela, E. I., Navarro, G., Franco, R. "Cocaine effects on dopaminergic transmission depend on a balance between sigma-1 and sigma-2 receptor expression." *Frontiers in Molecular Neuroscience* 11, article 17 (2018): 1-14; Rada, P., Avena, N. M., Hoebel, B. G. "Daily bingeing on sugar repeatedly releases dopamine in the accumbens shell." *Neuroscience* 134, no. 3 (2005): 737-744; Schultz, W., Dayan, P., Montague, P. R. "A neural substrate of prediction and reward." *Science* 275, no. 5306 (1997): 1593-1599.

25. Booker, K. "Extroverts have more sensitive brain-reward system." July 10, 2013. https://news.cornell.edu/stories/2013/07/brain-chemistry-plays-role-extroverts

26. Technically, a distinction exists between fear and anxiety, and it could be argued that much of what I refer to in this book is actually anxiety. I am guilty of this, and use the word fear as an umbrella term here.

27. While dopamine is most widely known for its association with rewards and pleasure, more recent evidence suggests it may play a role in fear as well: Brandão, M. L., Coimbra, N. C. "Understanding the role of dopamine in conditioned and unconditioned fear." Reviews in the Neurosciences 30, no. 3 (2019): 325-337.

28. Heinrichs, M., Baumgartner, T., Kirschbaum, C., Ehlert, U. "Social support and oxytocin interact to suppress cortisol and subjective responses to psychosocial stress." *Biological Psychiatry* 54, no. 12 (2003): 1389-1398; Kosfeld, M., Heinrichs, M., Zak, P. J., Fischbacher, U., Fehr, E. "Oxytocin increases trust in humans." *Nature* 435, no. 7042: (2005): 673-676.

29. Harvard TH Chan School of Public Health "Stress and Health." Accessed January 5, 2022. https://www.hsph.harvard.edu/nutritionsource/stress-and-health/; Kandhalu, P. "Effects of cortisol on physical and psychological aspects of the body and effective ways by which one can reduce stress." *Berkeley Scientific Journal* 18, no. 1 (2013): 14-16.

30. Heinrichs, M., Baumgartner, T., Kirschbaum, C., Ehlert, U., 1389-1398.

31. Uvnäs-Moberg, K., Handlin, L., Petersson, M. "Self-soothing behaviors with particular reference to oxytocin release induced by non-noxious sensory stimulation." *Frontiers in Psychology* 5, no. 1529 (2015): 1-16.

32. Kahneman, D., Deaton, A. "High income improves evaluation of life but not emotional well-being." *Proceedings of the National Academy of Sciences* 107, no. 38 (2010): 16489-16493.

33. Some of the early academic evidence of this was found by Kruger and Dunning (1999), whose results have more recently been argued to reflect a universal bias everyone has (Danvers 2020). (see Kruger, J., Dunning, D. "Unskilled and unaware of it: how difficulties in recognizing one's own incompetence lead to inflated self-assessments." *Journal of Personality and Social Psychology* 77, no. 6 (1999): 1121-1134; and Danvers, A. "Dunning-Kruger Isn't Real." *Psychology Today.* Dec 30, 2020. https://www.psychologyto-

day.com/us/blog/how-do-you-know/202012/dunning-kruger-isnt-real)

34. Significant differences exist across countries in how flexible both the education system and labor market are in allowing individuals to try out different career paths. However, the best time to explore remains immediately after finishing school, because the cost of switching careers typically increases with age.

35. There is, however, some reason to hope this might change. Programs like RULER, developed at the Yale Center for Emotional Intelligence, have shown promising results.

36. One could also argue that our theories of life are not, strictly speaking, good theories by scientific standards. One attribute of good theories is that they should be testable. I also admittedly make flexible use of the word theory in this book.

37. As one would expect, taking a passive approach to life is closely related to the philosophy one has about life.

38. See Reis, E. *The Lean Startup*. New York: Crown Business, 2011. Shapira (1995) also found in his study that the majority of managers viewed risk as something that could be controlled. (see Shapira, Zur. *Risk taking: A managerial perspective*. New York: Russell Sage Foundation, 1995.)

39. Since Maslow first published his hierarchy of needs in 1943, there has been subsequent debate about just how accurate the hierarchy structure itself is, and whether lower-level needs must be satisfied first before satisfying higher levels. For the discussion here, this issue is less relevant. What is important is the idea that universal human needs exist, which has been supported by more recent work. (see Maslow, A. H. "A theory of human motivation." *Psychological review* 50, no. 4 (1943): 370-396; Tay, L., Diener, E. "Needs and subjective well-being around the world." *Journal of Personality and Social Psychology* 101, no. 2 (2011): 354-365.)

40. To their credit, the British government has recognized the need for close human connection as a policy issue, creating a Minister of Loneliness position in 2018. Prompted by a dramatic increase in suicides, the Japanese government also created a similar position in 2021.

41. Fogel, A. "Emotional and Physical Pain Activate Similar Brain Regions." *Psychology Today.* April 19, 2012. https://www.psychologytoday.com/intl/blog/body-sense/201204/emotional-and-physical-pain-activate-similar-brain-regions

42. Csikszentmihalyi, M. *Flow: The psychology of optimal experience.* New York: HarperCollins, 1990.

43. Cranston, S., Keller, S. "Increasing the meaning quotient of work." *McKinsey Quarterly* 1 (2013): 48-59.

44. Steven Kotler, the Flow Research Collective, and other researchers have done, and continue to do, significant work to increase our understanding of flow.

45. Montessori schools are a notable exception to this.

46. Csikszentmihalyi, p. 3-4.

JANUARY
CAME

NICOLETTE A. EASLY

Book Cover Design: Prize Publishing House

Printed by: Prize Publishing House, LLC
in the United States of America.

First printing edition 2023.

Prize Publishing House
P.O. Box 9856, Chesapeake, VA 23321

www.PrizePublishingHouse.com

Library of Congress Control Number: 2023918566

ISBN (Paperback): 979-8-9892479-2-9
ISBN (E-Book): 979-8-9892479-3-6